UNMOVABLE

LESSONS FROM A BROKEN SUPERMAN

ROY WILLIAMS

WITH ANDREW MARTIN

CEDAR GATE
PUBLISHING

Cedar Gate Publishing
www.cedargatepublishing.com

ISBN: 979-8-9876329-9-4

To the people who saw me when I didn't see myself,
thank you for pushing me to become a better person.

And to those of you out there who don't think you have a voice,
let me be the first one to tell you that you do.

Be brave, be **UNMOVABLE.**

CONTENTS

ACHNOWLEDGMENTS i

CHAPTER 1 | OVERCOMING 1

CHAPTER 2 | STREETBALL 13

CHAPTER 3 | PEACE IN THE STORM. 25

CHAPTER 4 | VARSITY 35

CHAPTER 5 | WHATEVER IT TAHES 47

CHAPTER 6 | HARD WORK 57

CHAPTER 7 | READY 65

CHAPTER 8 | SUPERMAN 77

CHAPTER 9 | THE DRAFT. 103

CHAPTER 10 | AMERICA'S TEAM 113

CHAPTER 11 | UNMOVABLE 123

ACKNOWLEDGMENTS

To my mom, my hero! Thank you for believing in me and igniting the fire within me to become who I am today. I love you, Mom.

To my amazing kids, I love you. My hope is that you all find what you love to do and pursue it. Be great, be unmovable.

To our family's rock, my wife, Kristy Ann. Thank you for being in my life. Who would have thought that the same kid who used to put pencils and pens in your hair would one day be your husband? I am forever grateful to you. How much do I love you? Enough to admit that I have been a horrible person to you at times, but you saw the good in me anyway and accepted me as your husband.

To all my coaches, from little league to the pros, thank you for pushing me beyond my limits. The way I played was a result of your influence.

To Ms. B, there isn't enough paper to express my gratitude. Thank you for not giving up on me, for seeing me, and for continuing to fight for me. It meant a lot to me. You were a beacon of light in my dark world

To my Uncle Leander, you're the man! You have always been one of my biggest supporters. Thank you for always being there for me. Love you!

To my dad, I know this book doesn't portray our relationship in a perfect light. Just know that I love you so much and all I ever wanted was to feel that I made you proud.

To my guy Rod P! This book came to life because of you. When the Most High put it on your heart to approach me about telling my story, you listened. Thank you for joining me on this journey and walking beside me. You truly have seen all aspects of me and helped me connect with the people who have shaped me into the person I am today. Love you, dude! Thank you, thank you, thank you for believing in me and being a brother and friend.

To Andrew! You are truly a stud. Thank you for bringing my journey to life in this book. You were a true blessing to work with. Thank you for your patience with me. You are a gem, and I can't thank you enough for capturing my story. I look forward to our next adventure, my man.

— Roy

CHAPTER 1
OVERCOMING

I failed.

I thought I could do it. I felt like my life of classroom failures had just led me to this point.

The letters jumbled together like ancient hieroglyphics, and even though I knew them, they were always so unreadable.

Maybe I couldn't do it. Maybe it was just too hard.

Sitting at that tiny desk, I felt the room closing in around me. With another all-too-familiar test packet in front of me, I tapped my pencil on my desk as the teacher routinely gave the instructions like a flight attendant before takeoff. I didn't even know the difference between an SAT and an ACT, but here I sat ready to fill in some more bubbles.

The auditorium was packed like sardines with kids from all over the Bay Area. All of them hopeful, just like me, that we had studied enough, prepared enough, practiced enough. Our futures hung in the balance.

All I needed was a good enough score to secure my acceptance letter into a D1 school that wanted me to play football for them, but after taking the ACT three times already and failing to achieve the needed score each time, I now waged war against the doubt seeping through my mind. My future was on the chopping block. Even though there was not a single empty chair in that cavern of a room, I felt like I was the only one there.

Sweat slowly dripped down my forehead. The sound of the

teacher's voice was muddled as my mind raced. *Can I even pass this? I don't know. Will I ever be successful?*

"You may begin." Her voice interrupted my negative thoughts.

Like a drummer, I spun the pencil in my hand so I could use the eraser to break the seal on the packet. The smell of fresh paper popped into my senses as I flipped it back around and turned the sharpened lead back to the business at hand.

I had been here before. The first time I faced down a test packet was when I took the SAT, and back then, I just knew I was hot shit. I probably said something like, "I could take this stupid test with my eyes closed." But I had absolutely no idea what I was doing. By the time I got through the first half of the test, I had given up and started using the bubbles to create designs on the answer sheet. Needless to say, I bombed it.

Like a stray cow, I had been pushed through the school system from grade to grade to grade. I was a great football player, maybe the best, but I couldn't read. Somehow that hadn't mattered.

For as long as I can remember, the letters on the page constantly played tricks on me. The adults called it dyslexia, but I called it my life.

When I was in first grade, sitting at a desk much like where I found myself now, only smaller, my teacher, Mrs. Smith, sweetly led my classmates and me through our morning activities. Every day since the first day, she directed our attention to the gigantic calendar on the wall by the door. I can still hear her voice.

"Let's read it together, class."

We weren't actually reading, of course; we didn't know how to yet. But like a Mr. Miyagi who teaches wax on, wax off, she was teaching us about how letters worked together to form words, and subtly she was showing us that A-U-G-U-S-T spells August every single time or S-E-P-T-E-M-B-E-R is always September.

It took a while for me to really comprehend what I was seeing. But when all my friends began to see what she was saying, at some juncture I realized that I was only saying what she was saying. Because when I looked at the calendar, I didn't see the letters in the same order. No matter how hard I tried, no matter how many times I tried to blink my eyes to reset my brain, it never worked. What's more, the letters jumbled into a different order every time I looked at them. One time I would see U-A-G-S-U-T, and the next I would see A-G-U-U-T-S.

So, I did what every other self-respecting and completely em-barrassed five-year-old would do: I said nothing. And I continued to repeat what she said, even though I could never see what she saw.

Every time I tried and failed, my self-esteem took another hit. All my peers were learning to read, and I was just learning how to fake it. I was the youngest in my class, and I felt like I was constantly behind. No matter how hard I tried, I couldn't get it. At first, I really wanted to learn, but as time went on, my actual desire waned more and more.

"A. E. I. O. U."

I can still hear all our little voices sounding off simultaneously in our teacher's direction.

School was like my own little torture chamber. The more pain-ful it became, the more I found other ways to deal with it. Every class has a clown, and my class had me. I was funny, and I knew it. When my untimely comedy didn't satisfy the lingering desire to fit in that rolled around in my heart, I turned to all acts of disruption.

It didn't matter what my teachers tried. I was hell on wheels. They did try, though, most of them. It wasn't until fourth grade with Mrs. Hannah that I really felt motivated by a teacher to really try. She was incredibly easy on my young eyes. For a nine-year-old, I thought I was pretty hot stuff. So it felt normal to admit that I had a huge crush on her. She was like a model movie star who just happened to be my teacher. How could I not like her? But she was much more than just a pretty face: Unlike any teacher before, she figured out how to get through to me. Every time I actually applied myself, she would reward me with peanuts. She tried. Harder than the rest. But not even peanuts could steer me straight.

My family dynamic was messy, at best. Mom was and is the most incredible human being I could have ever asked to be raised by. The fact that Mom was always gone for work never fazed me much. She woke up early and got home after dark most nights. I knew about the sacrifices she was making to help provide opportunities for my sister and me. Mom had led the charge for us to leave Mountain View when our family moved north and across the bridge to Union City. She never gave the move a second thought, even though her job at the hospital by Stanford University would be nearly an hour's drive each way. The neighborhood and the school district promised to be better for my sister and me in Union City, so the move was a no-brainer for Mom.

"Son, I'll be home later. Remember there's a tuna casserole in the fridge for when you get home after school."

My stomach was always growling by the time the bell rang. She knew it, and so most days she got up earlier than she had to in order to make sure that I was taken care of.

On the other hand, my father was present and absent all at the same time. He made money so that food could be put on the table but never had much interest in being a part of our lives. I would catch him sometimes, just glaring in my direction. Those stares always felt as heavy as a ton of bricks. Their weight was composed of disapproval mixed with anger and a possible side of jealousy. I never knew if he was angry at me, Mom, or himself. He was never supportive, never outwardly loving, and never appreciative.

It was painful because all I wanted was to feel loved by my father. I loved and felt loved by my mom, but every son needs his dad. My heart ached daily. The pain was almost too much. If it had not been for my mom and football, I might never have made it.

It felt like I couldn't turn to anyone for help, but that was my own fault. Ashamed of what I was walking through, just like that *self-respecting and completely embarrassed five-year-old* I had been back in first grade, I continued to keep my adversity under wraps. I kept it a secret for too long, refusing to ask for help.

I know if I had asked, Mom would have been there for me in a heartbeat. I just never told her what was going on.

As junior year came, so did my first ACT test. I was hoping it would show me that, despite my struggle in school, I was doing alright. But no such luck. The score I got back was so low that it felt like a slap in the face.

Finally, I was sick of it. Sick of being constantly out of the loop. It was time to do something about it. They say the first step toward solving a problem is admitting that you have one. I had one. So, at last, I went to my mom.

"Mom, we need to talk."

Worry came over her face. As I grabbed her hand, my shadow enveloped hers while we made our way from the kitchen to the living room. Dad was gone as usual, but I didn't mind because I knew this conversation was for her ears only.

I led her to the couch so she could sit down before I dropped the nuclear warhead on her. With Dad living so absent all the time, I was always the stand-in "man of the house." Even though I didn't always show it, I felt responsible to watch over Mom. I didn't know it then, but I have since realized that part of the reason I was keeping my struggles to myself was so that I could protect her. But bombing the SAT and the ACT test, with no real answer to give for why I had done so poorly, pushed me over the edge.

"I can't read, Mom."

"What do you mean? You can't read?"

Tears welled in her eyes and started their slow-motion trek down her cheeks. With both hands, she tucked her curly black hair behind her ears. Brushing away the stream of tears, she turned to look at me.

Our eyes locked, and we just sat there for a long time.

Still holding my hand, she spoke gently. "Talk to me, son."

Over the next five excruciating minutes, all the secrets that I had been hiding about my struggles to overcome my learning disability began to flow out of my mouth. It was like her statement, "Talk to me, son," was the dynamite that finally broke the dam.

Then when she was completely up to speed with all of my struggles, she sandwiched my hand in between hers, locked her gaze with mine, and licked her lips.

"We're going to get through this. Together."

So, I put everything, all the simple pleasures of spending time with family and playing with friends, on the back burner. I didn't tell them what I was doing. I couldn't risk them knowing and thinking less of me. I spent every moment possible with tutors because I wasn't going to be pushed through the system anymore.

I learned something incredibly powerful in that moment with my mom on the couch. It's OK to ask for help. No matter how strong you think you are or how weak you think you will be perceived, it's OK to ask for help.

Mom was able to connect the dots between me and the tutors that I would need to finally be successful. First, we got connected with Miss Taylor, who lived on the Palo Alto side of the bridge. She was going to help me learn how to read. Miss Taylor and I met two days a week for a full year.

Then after I had learned how to read, I stopped meeting with Miss Taylor and started with Miss Judy. Thankfully, she lived on our side of the bridge in Fremont, and she was going to help me study for the ACT specifically. Just like I had with Miss Taylor, I met with Miss Judy two days a week.

All the while, Mom would drive the almost-hour home from work, pick me up, and take me wherever I needed to go. A twenty- or forty-minute drive, not counting traffic. It was a sacrifice that she was willing to make.

Both of my tutors taught me so much. I learned multiple lessons that would stay with me forever. Three of those lessons catapulted me far past the ACT and into my future.

"It's OK to not know that answer."

"Don't let this struggle define you."

"If you look, there is strength to be found in the struggle."

When I started my junior year, I was given a gift—at least, that's what I like to say she was. Ms. B was a game changer. She was my eleventh- and twelfth-grade teacher, and of all the teachers I had ever experienced, she was the best.

Tina Bobadilla was just a young, tiny Filipino woman with a heart the size of Cowboys Stadium.

Every morning she stood at her door waiting to greet us. She would stare up into my eyes without ever breaking her glance. After lifting her right hand, she kindly pressed her right index finger into my chest. "Roy." Then she would pause for what seemed like forever. "I'm not going to let you fail."

Between my mom, Miss Judy, Miss Taylor, and Ms. B, my chances improved greatly.

Toward the end of my junior year, I took my second ACT test, and then my third test during my first semester as a senior. My scores were certainly improving, but they were still beneath the benchmark I needed.

When it came time to take it a fourth time, I had been working with Miss Judy for almost two and a half years.

I was determined to make this time different.

"Five more minutes." The teacher's announcement shook me back into the present where I sat taking my fourth ACT in that cavern of a room.

I looked at my answer card to see all the little lead-colored-in bubbles looking back at me.

I passed. It wasn't perfect, but it was enough.

Colleges from everywhere were already recruiting me. I don't know how they got my mom's address, but every day there were more letters in the mail. I wanted to take my football career to the next level. UCLA, USC, Notre Dame, Nebraska, and Oklahoma all wanted me to become the next big playmaker in their program. Recruiting letters by the dozen filled our mailbox at home and at the coach's office daily. Passing the ACT gave me a confidence that I had never had before.

My future was finally in front of me. Overcoming might really be possible. A life beyond the hexagon might not just be a passing dream but a reality in the making.

Above all, there's one lesson Miss Judy taught me in all those hours of studying for the ACT that I'll never forget. A lesson that equipped me as I went to college, that found its way onto the football field, and that helped me to grow in every area of life.

In the ACT, there are four main sections: English, mathematics, reading, and science. Each one of those sections contains its own list of sixty or so questions, and each one of those questions has its own steps you have to go through to answer it. But if you're like me, all of that tends to blur together in your mind, and you get lost in a sea of half-answered questions.

So, using a sample test, Miss Judy pointed to a single question.

"Don't worry about the next section, the next question, or the next step in the problem. Get all of that out of your head, and just focus on the step in front of you. Break it down into little pieces."

She smiled as she handed me the pencil, and then said, "To take it down, you have to break it down."

Mrs. Bobadilla Story

CHAPTER 2
STREETBALL

Life at 4207 Solar Circle was home. Then when we moved across the street to 4212, from garage to garage, we really put down our family roots. At the same time, our hexagonal prison-like neighborhood in Union City held me captive, making me believe from a young age that this was it. There was nothing outside of my present, no opportunities for a kid like me. I was destined to remain right where I was. In spite of being enslaved to wrong mindsets, I would never change a thing about my childhood. There were a hundred kids within walking distance, and I knew all of them. They were my classmates, my teammates, my potential girlfriends, my best friends, and my enemies. Our neighborhood was called Contempo, three full circles lined with townhomes inside and out. In elementary school they were dark brown with light brown trim, and then about the time puberty brought all its drastic changes, the homes got a makeover too. No matter their color, they housed people from every background and too many nationalities to count. They were more than just a bunch of houses: they were our stadium, our playground, our practice field, and our training ground for life.

Years before the ACT, when I was just a kid, football was my escape from the difficulty that I experienced every day in the classroom. I have been playing since before I can remember. In Contempo we had neighborhood boys of every age. It didn't matter if you were young or old, in elementary or high school—we all played all out. No-holds-barred, full-contact football. Before I ever got my first real jersey, I had been hit so many times I lost count. Lloyd Greenwood was both an opponent and an occasional team-mate. He was a mountainous seventeen-year-old offensive lineman on the high school varsity team, and way too big for me to tackle. But that never stopped me from trying.

"Ha ha ha ..."

His deep-voice laughter would ring in my ears for days after he plowed over me.

 **Lloyd Greenwood Story**

But I kept trying. I studied my mistakes as much as I took note of my successes. Every failed attempt at tackling the bigger guys would play over and over in my dreams. Eventually, I learned that if I tried to hit him high, he would just trample me. If I tried to take him out at the knees, he would use his powerful legs to knock me backward. But if I went for his ankles, even though I was so much smaller, I could wrap him up enough that even the giant would fall.

I was a self-taught tackler. Tackling is definitely not for the faint of heart. You have to WANT to learn. I was just six years old facing boys ten years my senior, but I WANTED to learn.

It was a beautiful California day, perfect for a game of football in the street. We just called it streetball. It required quickness, in-stincts, a smile, and a healthy portion of stupidity (enough at least to play a full-contact sport in the middle of the street where there were cars parked and moving).

The sun was shining, and a slight western breeze carried with it a faint salty scent from the bay. We had already picked teams, and the rough-and-tumble game that we all loved was about to kick off. Damian was my boy—my best friend—but on that morning, we were playing opposite sides of the ball.

Sweat dripped from our bodies, and our knees and elbows were almost perpetually scraped and bruised.

Streetball was not for the faint of heart.

Cars didn't mark the out-of-bounds line: They were teammates and blockers and occasionally fierce opponents. When you got tackled or hit by a car, you remembered it. What I was learning in the street and in the hexagon of my neighborhood was conditioning a toughness in me that could not have been developed otherwise. I was being built into the player that I would become.

When we weren't playing streetball, we took our team on the road. It was my first travel team. All the boys who were around my age from my neighborhood formed a team, and we would walk anywhere and play anybody. Sometimes we played at home on our own turf, but a lot of the time we walked almost a mile away, crossing some major roads just to get to the other team's field.

At home, we had an old life jacket that I used as football pads. The life preserver went around my neck, and the front part was like a breastplate. We lived in a neighborhood that was landlocked, so I don't even know why we had a life jacket, but we did, and I put it to use on a regular basis.

Putting on that life jacket teleported me into my own football Narnia-like world. I ran around my parent's house, all 1,280 square feet of it, just as if I were playing before eighty thousand fans. I didn't see a dresser or a doorway. I saw an A-gap (the space between the center and the guard) and a B-gap (the space between the guard and the tackle). Pumping my arms, I would run through the gaps before the defensive linemen could tackle me. The game was real to me. The doorway faded into two guys attacking me on the line. At the snap of the next down, I'd run and dive onto my mom and dad's bed for a touchdown. Hands raised above my head in celebration, I had no way of knowing how well my play was foreshadowing my future.

First Tackle Football Game

I was an unstoppable force, but I hadn't always been like that. Mom always said I was a determined little baby and a rambunctious kid. She first noticed my strength when I learned to walk at just ten months old.

"Both my babies were early walkers," she used to tell people.

I was born pigeon-toed and had club feet as a baby. I was so bowlegged I looked like a cowboy after a long hard day's ride in the old West. It ran in the family. My grandmother on my dad's side was bowlegged as well. About the time I started walking, Mom took me to the doctor to see what could be done to fix my legs and feet. Since she knew about the family history, she was willing to do anything to make sure that I could get it taken care of early in my development. The doctor fitted me with special shoes that were designed to straighten my legs. There wasn't a right and a left shoe, but both shoes were identical. They were straight, stiff, and white. A bar that connected the two together should have made it impossible for the ten-month-old or even two-year-old me to move in the crib at night. But not even that bar could hold me back.

Every night went the same. When it was time for me to go to bed, Mom would say, "Come here, babe, let's put your shoes on."

If she hadn't made me, I wouldn't have worn them. I hated them. They were terribly uncomfortable. It was like I had to put my little feet back in prison every night.

From a very early age, I loved to run even though it took a long time for me to really find my stride. I'm so thankful for how Mom reacted to those beginning signs. I know now that she had no clue about how big of an impact sports would have on my life. But because she wanted me to have the best chance possible, she made a way.

Football was what kept me busy and, for the most part, out of trouble in my adolescence. There was a group of us boys from my neighborhood who all played. Those days in Contempo were the best. We had access to all the gaming systems available: Sega, Super Nintendo, PlayStation, and Nintendo 64. But most of the time we still chose to play outside. The plum or cherry trees in our neighborhood were great climbing trees. We'd climb up just high enough to knock the fruit off, and then we'd take our loot and run to hide somewhere that we could eat in peace.

When I was eight years old, I told my mom about a local Pop-Warner League where I could finally play organized football. She could see how badly I wanted to play. More than anyone else, she had noticed the bumps and bruises that I had come home with from streetball or games in the hexagonal playground with the big boys.

So, against my father's wishes, my mom took me to sign-ups. Getting that first red jersey with black lettering and our Union City Colts logo, just like the high school team jerseys, was better than any Christmas or birthday gift I had ever received. It really was a gift that kept giving. Then she took me to the local sporting goods store and bought me my first pair of cleats, black Nike Sharks. When I made the team, I got my pants, pads, and helmet. I was ready for war.

Coming home that day with all my new gear, all I wanted was for my dad to be excited for me, but he never looked up from his chair. Inwardly, I was hurt, but outwardly no one knew. Unashamedly, I wore that red Union City Colts jersey everywhere.

I was ready to play before we even had our first practice.

"Let's go, Colts!"

The cheers from the stands on that first scrimmage are etched in my memory forever. We had traveled that morning to San Jose. The sun was shining, a perfect day for football. The smell of the green grass filled my nostrils.

This was a first-year team: If my teammates had played any football before, it was probably just in their local parks and front yards. So, we were all just learning—at least, that's what my mom said. But not me. I had been playing for a lifetime before my eighth birthday. I was pumped!

We had practiced. We had learned. We were ready.

"Roy, you're gonna play halfback today."

I knew I would before the game even started because I had been practicing all week. But I also knew Coach could always change his mind. So, when he told me, I knew that I had the trust of my coaches and my teammates. I also knew that I had a huge responsibility. This was not just an opportunity to take the ball and run with it. It was my job and my duty to get the ball and hold on to it.

I could hear his screaming voice from practice and repeat in my mind.

"Don't drop the ball! Hold on to that ball, son!"

On our first possession, Coach called a lead play.

All of the moments of being bullied by the ball carriers of previous games in the street flashed into my mind as we broke from the huddle. Now it was my turn.

"Down. Set. Hut! Hut!"

As I got the hand-off, everything blurred from my vision. All I could see was red. Everything I had learned from playing with Greenwood and the guys, every time I had gotten hit, crushed, dog-piled, and run over, echoed in my every neuron. From a very early age, I had learned to play with anger.

That "Oh, you're about to get it" attitude gives a bigger boost than any energy drink on the market.

With the ball tucked deep underneath my arm, I blasted through the gap.

In an instant I saw him, the kid standing in my way. My eyes zoomed in on him like there was a target on his chest.

My legs were pumpin'. I lowered my shoulder and aimed my helmet directly at the target. He wasn't ready for what was about to happen. But I knew.

Pop!

That sound that a helmet makes when it connects with its target is unlike any other.

As soon as I felt his arms come forward and his chest sink in like a crash dummy right after impact, I shot my head upward, flipping him. In a crazy moment that moved so fast and so slow at the same time, I watched him all the way through the air to the place where he crashed into the field. Then I saw my opportunity, my chance to finally do what had been done to me. With anger runnin' through my veins, I ran right over the top of him, making sure to take a few extra steps on his chest.

With that kid in my dust, there was nothing and no one standing in my way of the end zone. Even if there had been, I would've run them over too.

"Touchdown!" The announcer's voice interrupted my trance.

My team surrounded me in the end zone.

Out of the corner of my eye, I could see that the golf cart ambulance was making its way onto the field to check on the kid I had just run over.

Coach was high-fiving me as I came off the field. I glanced up into the stands to see if my mom was as excited as I was. But she had an angry look on her face, and she was making her way toward me.

When she made it down to the sideline, I took my helmet off so that I could face her.

"Roy. You can't be doin' that!"

"Mom, I just scored."

"No, you just ran that little boy over! And now ... you're going to go apologize."

My look of disgust and disagreement was not what she wanted from me. I couldn't believe that she wanted me to apologize. It's a good thing she couldn't hear my thoughts. *This is football. You don't apologize in football. This is stupid!*

Mom didn't say a word. She just pointed in the direction of the boy who was now lying on the back of the little golf cart ambulance. They were preparing to cart him off and take him to the ER. It looked pretty serious.

Reluctantly, I jogged over in his direction.

He stared up at me.

"Hey," I started. "My mom wanted me to come over here and tell you I'm sorry."

My expression probably didn't match my words, and my tone

was probably a little sarcastic. But Mom couldn't hear me from the sidelines.

Nowadays, lowering your helmet is definitely frowned upon, and flipping people on their backs with head-to-head contact is illegal. But back then, it was just part of the full-contact sport I was falling in love with.

Mom had tried other sports before finally giving in and signing me up for battle on the gridiron. First, it had been T-ball. But I hated it almost instantly. It was too slow. But Mom was just trying to get me into something that would burn off all my energy.

Then it was basketball. St. Anne's was a church around the corner from our house, and they had a league for kids my age. The problem with basketball was that I liked to hit people. Whenever they put me in, I would have three or four fouls in like three seconds. But when I finally asked my Mom about football, she always said that when she gave her consent, my eyes lit up with the right kind of excitement. The kind that her motherly instincts knew was for real. Ultimately, it was that moment between my mom and me that compelled her to get me on my first football team. Maybe it was that moment that encouraged her to let me continue to play, even after I ran over that kid on my first possession.

I needed football, and in a lot of ways, football needed me. The instant that Mom signed me up for the first time was the epic moment that would change my life forever. Football helped me become me. It required so much from me, but I gave my all, and as a result it shaped me both mentally and physically.

Football was my life. I played in that Pop-Warner league from when I was eight years old until I finished my eighth-grade year. I even made the All-Star team multiple times. Making the All-Star team was such a big deal. I remember the moment that I heard my thoughts. I made it. I am gonna get to play with the best of the best.

I can still hear Coach's instruction: "Alright, boys, we're going to make a video that will play before the game. Come up to the camera and just introduce yourself."

With all the coaches watching, we did as we were instructed. All sixty of us went walking up to a camera to shoot our video. Straight-faced, actin' like we were older than we were.

"I'm Roy Williams, number thirty, for the Union City Colts." Without breaking my tough-guy face, I walked away from the camera. I was just nine years old at the time.

Three-time all-star and three championships in my first four years were pretty incredible. Sure, it was just pee-wee football, but it was the foundation that I didn't know my life would be built on. I didn't realize how important those years were then. But I was learning everything I would need to know for life inside that 100-yard field. Life wasn't easy. Practice was grueling. School sucked continuously. My father was almost totally checked out, except for when it came to my occasional need for corporal punishment.

But my mom was consistently for me. My teammates, both on the street and on the field, were always with me. And football was constantly building me.

CHAPTER 3
PEACE IN THE STORM

It was a beautiful Easter Sunday in California. The sun was shining. Not a single cloud in the sky. Alone, I was out in the backyard by the pool. Our family had driven to a neighboring town for Sunday dinner at Diane and Larry's house in Hayward. (Diane was my mom's friend.)

When we first arrived at the house, Diane had warned me: "Roy, don't you go near that pool in your church clothes."

Then Mom and the family went inside.

But my mind was where it usually is—the football field. Junior high was flying by. The thing that had not changed was that my mind was constantly thinking about the last game. Stewing over all that I had done well and all that I could improve on. Thinking over that hit that I put on #83 in our last game or that hit I took down the street last night.

I didn't even recognize how close a line I was walking near the edge of the pool. All it took was one wrong step. Before I could catch myself, in a slow-motion move, a little like when I ran over that kid so many years before, I fell into the pool.

"I can't swim!" I screamed.

But no one was there to hear me.

In the next few seconds, everything moved a million miles an hour and slower than a turtle all at the same time. My mind slipped into silence as I sank to the bottom of the ocean-like pool. Blue water enveloped me as I began struggling to get to the surface. The more I struggled, the more I stayed right where I was.

Sinking.

But in a moment where I should have been freaking out, completely and totally bothered by my inability to make my situation better, a strange calm swept over me. I almost came to peace with knowing this might be it. This might be my end. With no one around to even know about my demise, I knew that I might die right here at the bottom of the pool.

Still, there was something deep inside of me that refused to give up. Without knowing what I was doing, I moved my arms just so, and magically I went forward. I did it again and again, and then instinctively I kicked my feet a little like a frog. I was swimming.

I made it. I gasped for air when I finally broke the surface.

I lived.

Even still, the realization that I could've died wasn't the biggest "aha" that I got that day. The "aha" came in the form of a lesson that I wouldn't even realize I had learned until years later in high school.

Shock had taken over my body. Wet from head to toe, I stumbled toward the house. My shoes made that unmistakable squishing sound as I walked through the back door.

The sound of the dripping of water hitting the floor interrupted the conversation in the living room. Heads turned slowly.

Diane reacted first. "Roy! What were you thinking?"

Then Mom chimed in. "You know you can't swim!"

They weren't mad at me but upset that I was so careless with how close I had gotten to the pool. Even more so, I know they were puzzled at how I was acting. The euphoria of the peace that I experienced at the bottom, just before I taught myself how to swim, hadn't worn off.

I couldn't help it. I was just completely unmovable. It was how I lived.

Soon enough, the grindstone of Monday would shake me back to the reality of my present. The routine of upper elementary and junior high was horrible. One of the only ways I made it through the grades was by acting out as a class clown. I was funny, or at least I thought I was. The teachers never saw it that way. The disruption I regularly caused became too much. What they didn't know was that my dyslexia and my inability to read ruled my life in the classroom. The only way I could feel good about my situation was to joke about it.

Almost drowning was more than a little bit of a wake-up call. I tried to be better. Tried to focus more on being good in the classroom instead of always cutting up. But it didn't last for long. Mom tried multiple times to confront me about my behavior. Those were some really tough conversations between her and me. She never gave up on me, but at some point, she had to tell the teachers to stop calling her. Mom drove an hour one way to work every day, and that's not counting the extra time it took if the traffic was bad. And traffic in the Bay Area is almost always bad.

"I can't keep coming up to the school every time he does something," she told them. "Tell him that you're going to call his dad."

Threatening to call Dad definitely worked when I was younger. He told me one time, "Roy, if I have to, I will come up to that school and beat your butt in front of whoever is standing around."

I knew he would too. He wouldn't hesitate to embarrass me in front of everybody.

As I got older, the threat of my dad started to lose its power. At some point, I heard Mom tell one of my teachers, "You're just going to have to deal with it."

It was almost like my teachers had a secret meeting where they brainstormed together to figure out the quickest way to get me out of their hair. I'm sure they probably didn't actually have a meeting, but they all seemed to have the same idea. The only way they could get me out of their classroom was to graduate me to the next grade. Fifth grade, sixth grade, seventh grade, eighth grade, and so on I went. Advancing because I was a problem child instead of on the basis of my ability to progress.

When I wasn't struggling in the classroom, I always had plenty of football things to keep my mind off of it all. It seemed like every afternoon, Imoni, our self-appointed neighborhood coach, had a different drill planned for me. Imoni was the same age as my sister, out of school already, and living on the corner of our neighborhood. Most of the time, when he wanted to work with us, he made us do the one-yard-line drill.

"Roy, you're on defense!" His voice was abrupt and loud.

"Now, Moose, you line up against him."

Mustafa was my buddy. Unlike Greenwood, Moose was pretty close to me in age, but he was still way bigger than I was. His short and stocky build made him quite the opponent for the drill that Imoni put us through.

"Listen up, boys!"

Our heads slowly turned to face him. Imoni took his job seriously, and for the most part we had learned to take him seriously. The instructions were always the same.

"Roy, you better not let Moose score!"

Roy v Moose

Then in the same breath, he would turn to face Moose. "Moose, you better run him over!"

At his command, the one-yard fight would be on. Moose could drive his legs like a pro. But even as a middle schooler, I was no slouch on the defensive side of the ball. With my heels up on the curb, I would hold him with all my might. All the while, Imoni would be yelling at both of us to win our respective positions.

Sometimes Moose won. Other times, I won. We fought a lot of one-yard battles with Imoni shouting over our shoulders. He was like our own Dumbledore, always teaching us lessons about toughness without ever saying anything.

One thing about Imoni: he had some strange techniques for sure.

I had to walk past his house on the way to the bus stop in the morning. One day as I walked past, daydreaming about anything but school, I heard them just over my shoulder. Imoni's pit bulls.

"Run!" he screamed from behind me.

There were two of them, and they were fast.

Imoni must have thought it was helping with my speed, or maybe with my ability to be fearless. He must've because he didn't let them chase me once or twice, but three times. Every time, he screamed over my shoulder for me to run faster.

The first time I evaded them by jumping onto a gray electrical box. The kind that acts as a hub for all the electricity in a neighborhood. The second time, I ran a bit farther before they were breathing on my ankles. I made my escape when I jumped onto a parked car.

By the third time, I was sick and tired of being chased. The worst part was that I knew that Imoni was trying to teach me something again. But I was tired of trying to figure out what it was. I had run far enough, enough times.

I turned around midstride, with absolutely no idea of exactly what I was going to do next.

The dogs never stopped. They were bearing down on me, like Moose did in the one-yard drill.

Pop!

Almost without thinking about it, I kicked the big dog, the one Imoni called Bag Lady, with all the power in my right leg. The sound my foot made when it connected with her jaw sounded just like my helmet did when I got a big hit. She tucked her tail and ran back toward home.

The Pit Bull Story

I watched as Bag Lady and the other dog ran down the street, and I finally understood what Imoni had been trying to teach me. A guy has got to learn how to stand up for himself, no matter what sort of opposition he is facing. On the field and off the field. And I needed to work on my speed.

As much as I loved football, it didn't consume my every moment. We played hide-and-seek around the neighborhood. Sometimes we would go down to the train tracks to walk around looking for lizards, money, or other treasures. One warm afternoon after school, I was walking through my neighborhood when I went by Omar's house. Occasionally, he and I played together. He wasn't on my everyday sandlot team, but he was pretty cool.

When I made the corner by his house, something strange

immediately caught my eye. It was him, but it wasn't just Omar that had caught my eye. He was standing beside a tree with a pellet gun pointed right at me.

"Dude, stop!"

He had done that before but never actually shot at me. This time would be different.

Holding the gun at his hip, he shifted his weight when I told him to stop, and he raised it to his shoulder like he was taking aim. The sun flashed off the barrel.

I wasn't going to stick around to see if he really meant to shoot. So I took off down the back alley. Just about the time I made it out of sight, I heard it.

Bang!

He pulled the trigger.

It was not the first time I had heard a gun go off in our neighborhood. The local authorities had built a temporary police station in our neighborhood because of how bad it was.

I wasn't sure if the bullet hit me, but he didn't stop firing even as I was running away.

A couple of weeks later, I remember walking by my dad in our house, rubbing my head. It was throbbing.

"Hey, boy, you OK?"

I wasn't OK. The bullet was rotting on the inside of my head and oozing a brown-yellow pus. I thought it was just a pimple.

Dad insisted I tell him what happened, and after I described what had gone down with Omar, he took me to the hospital.

When we told the on-call doctor about what had happened, he was immediately concerned, especially since the small bump was just behind my temple. They had to make a small incision, but what they found confirmed what I had hoped wasn't true. There was a pellet in my head. Just two inches away from my temple.

"Son, you're lucky," I remember the doctor saying. "If that pellet had hit your temple, your friend would've killed you."

They let me keep the pellet. But my dad gave me strict instructions.

"Take that pellet over to Omar's house and give it back to him. Tell him he almost killed you and that you can't be playin' with him anymore."

Omar and I went way back. He and I played Pop-Warner football together for the Union City Colts. I gave him the pellet and told him what my dad had told me to say. He didn't say much.

Getting shot made me feel like just another statistic in our neighborhood. I wasn't like that. I never did the things that most boys my age were doing because, despite my learning difficulties, I had a pretty good head on my shoulders.

Sure, it was just an air gun. But two inches forward, and I could've died.

My near-death experience gave me a new drive. No matter what, I would not quit. I couldn't. No matter what, I had to keep going. I had to be tougher than my age said I could be. I needed to be stronger than the next guy. Faster. Hungrier.

 **Roy Shot in the Head**

CHAPTER 4
VARSITY

*R*ing! Ring!

The tardy bell was my greeter every morning. If it had been football, I would have beaten the bell every day and been early, but school wasn't anything to rush for.

My freshman year was a bit of a blur. It was definitely an adjustment from junior high. We didn't have organized football in junior high back then. I still played on the Pop-Warner team. In addition to my organized team, I still spent a ton of time playing in the street or wherever we could find a good patch of grass and an opponent to play against. I was undersized when I started my ninth-grade year, only five foot six. But finally, I hit a growth spurt that summer and shot up to five ten.

Walking into the halls of my sophomore year, I felt like I had a brand-new lease on life in some ways. I was taller, and I had worked really hard that summer to be prepared to play past the JV squad.

One day, in the middle of summer football practice, the sun glistened off every helmet. Sweat dripped from every player like a leaky faucet. In the middle of a drill, the varsity head coach and I locked eyes. I'm pretty sure he was already looking in my direction when I finally caught on.

"Roy, you got a minute?" But he wasn't really looking for me to answer. He waved his hand over his right shoulder, motioning for me to follow him.

He led me inside and into the gymnasium. The lights were on, like he'd already been in there. We walked briskly until we were standing directly underneath the basketball goal.

"Coach?"

"Can you do it?" Pointing his finger upward, he flashed his eyes from me to the rim and back again.

I had been working hard all summer. Honestly, I didn't know if I could jump flat-footed and touch the rim or not. But I didn't really think about whether or not I could. I just jumped.

When I got three fingers on the rim on the first try, I'm not sure who was more surprised: me or Coach.

"Alright. So come back this afternoon at three o'clock sharp. You just made varsity."

I nodded my head in agreement, trying to contain my excitement as best I could. Then Coach Fromson just turned and walked out of the gym, leaving me with my thoughts. *I just grabbed the rim. Wait ... I just made varsity! I gotta tell somebody!*

Jogging out of the gym and back to the football field, where my junior varsity teammates were still in the middle of practice and wondering where I had disappeared to, I found Damian and some of the other guys.

"Yo, Coach said I'm gonna be on varsity!"

Their smiles and high-fives were just the kind of affirmation I needed right then. But there was one more person I had to tell.

I never had any money in my pocket for making phone calls, so anytime I needed to call my mom, I always called collect. Waiting till after our practice was over felt like cruel and unusual punishment.

"Hey, Mom," I began without warning, "the head football coach just told me I'm on varsity!"

There was a pause on the line for just a moment while the news set in. But I didn't let it linger.

"Yeah, so, I wanted to tell you because I wanted you to know, but also because I won't be home at the normal time because I'll be at practice. So can you pick me up?"

"Hey, no problem, babe. Just have fun, and ... please don't get hurt."

I was already the youngest kid in my class, so when I showed up for practice that day, I was literally the youngest guy on the field. My age didn't win me any favor with the guys either. From the first moment in the locker room, most of the older guys started to pick on me. But I had already been playing with older guys for so long, so their attempts to rile me up didn't really work.

When we finally got to our first scrimmage and I got to play, I knew I had to make the most of my opportunity to show the guys that age didn't matter.

Back in the day, the junior varsity team would always come to the games because they played right before us. They were required to sit up in the stands to watch varsity play. When we were on the defensive side of the ball and our opponent had someone open downfield for a pass, you could hear the JV team shout in unison from the stands.

"Pass! Pass!"

Then when the ball left the quarterback's hand, you could hear them again.

"Ball! Ball! Ball!"

As a defender, I had to be focused on my guy or the zone that I was responsible for covering. But when I heard them yell, "Ball," I knew I needed to be looking.

Eventually, you level up your spidey senses, and you don't need anyone to yell anything: You just know. But especially in those first few games, it was super helpful to have that extra edge from their point of view in the stands.

I spotted the ball as it moved through the air and flew past the beam of the stadium lights. Don't ask me how I know, but I just know where the ball is going when I see it. I can always tell by its trajectory. This is especially helpful when you play like I do. All I could see in that instant was the target on the back of the receiver who was about to catch the ball. Playing in the street and the hexagon had prepared me for this moment. Never hold back. Hit them as hard as possible. Time your impact. Make it hurt.

As the ball made its way down, I was running full steam ahead. Everything around blurred into an almost frozen slo-mo.

Then, just like when the wall suddenly meets the crash dummy...

Pop!

I had learned to aim just right so that when I hit them, their arms flail backward. Most of the time they drop the ball because of the shockwave that enters their body upon my arrival.

The crowd went nuts! "Boom!" someone yelled.

Knowing that play was their third down attempt, I jumped up to trot off the field.

My teammates were hoopin' and hollerin', but what really pumped me up was seeing how hyped my coach was.

That was the moment that Young Roy was born. That became the nickname that followed me for most of my high school career. I didn't care what they called me as long as Coach kept calling my number. After that hit, most of the older guys stopped picking on me.

When the regular season came, I had already secured my starting position on the field. It was time to hit some people, and I was ready.

The first game of our regular season that year, we faced Skyline High School. They had a highly touted wide receiver who Coach said we had to shut down if we wanted to secure our win.

On one of the first plays of their offensive sequence, they called a hitch-and-go route for him. I was on the backside of the play, lined up as a cornerback, on the opposite side of the field from him.

"Ball! Ball!" the JV team in the stands shouted.

But I had already noticed. I left my man in a full-on sprint cutting back across the field as soon as the quarterback released the ball. He was fast and slightly pulling away from our corner who was guarding him. We all knew who was going to get the ball anyway. The star player almost always gets the ball on the first play. With his hands outstretched for the reception and his eyes focused on the incoming football, he never saw me coming.

Pop!

"Ooooh ..." The crowd grimaced.

I laid him clean out. He was lucky his helmet didn't pop off.

We went on to win the game, and the star receiver never caught another pass.

And that was how my season went. From then on, my job was to deliver nonstop warzone kind of hits. The kind where the shockwave can be felt like a tidal-wave-sized ripple.

Even though I was still just a young guy, every time I made another big hit, I could tell that things on the team were shifting. Not only was I being accepted, but I was being welcomed. I found out that making varsity in the coach's eyes and being on varsity in my teammates' eyes were two totally different things. It felt really, really good. I knew I had finally made it when the older guys looked at me as their equal, even though I was only fifteen and nearly three years younger than most of them.

All those times when Lloyd Greenwood had run me over, and I was still just the six-year-old teaching myself how to tackle, were finally paying off. He had always been like my impossible opponent. But since I never believed in what I *couldn't do*, impossible was never in my vocabulary. Gradually, my hitting tactics were becoming second nature to me. I knew I had to break them down to take them down. And most of the time I was successful.

Most kids spend all their elementary years looking forward to being in high school. There's just something about it that seems so attractive when you're younger. But when I finally made it, even though the football was great, school still sucked.

But thankfully, football was so good that my constant struggle in the classroom was just something I tolerated during the day while I waited to go do the thing that I really came to school for. Football.

It wasn't until the summer of my sophomore year that I began to discover the lesson of the "aha" moment that I had experienced when a peace had washed over me at the bottom of Diane and Larry's pool. The nearly four years since almost drowning seemed like a lifetime ago. But when I was at the bottom, slowly running out of air, a single thought exploded in my mind.

There is always a way out.

It was that thought that led me past the imminent outcome of dying, drowning, and giving in to the water pressing all the oxygen out of my lungs. It was that thought that made me almost subconsciously move my arms just so, discovering a way to move forward.

As my sophomore year ended and summer came, I finally got the guts to go to my mom to talk about what had been happening in school since the first grade.

There are so many lessons that I learned as I studied that summer with Miss Judy and Miss Taylor. Primary among them was that if you are not willing to ask for help, then you don't really believe that there is a way out.

Ever so slowly, the reading light bulb was coming on for me. Putting everything and everyone on hold for the summer so that I could pursue learning for the first time ever was difficult. But I knew that the difficulty would pay off, just like it had for my game. I had already tried to take the ACT once and failed. What I began to discover was that the only thing standing in the way of me becoming me was the brain between my two ears. I couldn't risk not knowing because as much as I will always be afraid of drowning, I have always been more afraid of letting my people down.

I had already gotten a few recruiting letters as a sophomore. But they were generic. Sometimes my boy Damian and I would compare letters and find that he and I got the exact same one. The only thing that was different was that they had changed his name to mine or mine to his.

"Yo, Damian, do you think they're even real?"

"The letters? Nah, I don't think so."

But having failed the ACT once also got the attention of Fresno State University. I had already gotten phone calls from their head coach who let me know that it was OK if I *couldn't* pass the ACT. He could get me a chance anyway.

"Just let me know," he had said. "We'd love to have you here at Fresno State."

But I didn't want to go to Fresno State. More than that, I didn't like hearing how he had said it: "*Couldn't pass.*" So I studied even harder. By the end of the summer, I could finally do something that I hadn't done my whole life. I could read. Besides learning how to read, I learned something even more valuable. My teachers deserved the same respect that I gave to my coaches. I had never thought about it like that, but I had never thrived in the teacher's environment and had always seen them as the opponent instead of the coach of my classroom. When our coach was hard on us on the field, I never got offended because I knew that he saw something in us to be greater. Miss Judy and Miss Taylor were constantly telling me that they could see something in me to be more. That's when I began to get the right perspective.

My counselor said it was time to take the ACT again, but I didn't think I was quite ready yet. So Miss Judy and I studied harder. With football starting back up, I had less time to work with her, but now, in eleventh grade, I also had Ms. B on my team.

No one knew it then, but my junior year would be my breakout year. It all started with our game against Pittsburg High.

It was not the safest place to go, but their team was amazing. When we arrived to play that day, we knew that Pittsburg had put up an impressive stand against undefeated De La Salle. No team ever stood a chance when they shared the field with the De La Salle Spartans, who went on to have a 151-game winning streak. There was a lot of talk from high school sports analysts that said Pittsburg was almost unbeatable. Their roster was jam-packed with stars, both present and future, including Ken Simonton (who would go on to be a leading rusher at Oregon State). They were highly ranked in our region and were expected to contend for the state championship. All that stood in their way was us.

The odds were stacked against us. They had everything any team would want. Home-field advantage. A stadium full of family, friends, and fans cheering them toward victory. The atmosphere was electric. I had never experienced anything quite like that before and may not have seen anything like it since.

Every school does something to hype up their players right before the kickoff. Even in my short high school career, I thought I'd seen everything there was to see. Pittsburg had a band, but not just any band. Every school has a band, but I'd never seen or heard anything like the Pittsburg High Marching Showband. The fight song was the most unique I had ever heard. Listening to them play and watching them get hyped to their own music was awesome.

But it also revealed just how normal our fight song was. I liked ours OK, but theirs had a hip-hop beat to it and almost sounded like something I would've chosen to listen to on the radio.

Without even thinking about it, I was really groovin' to the music that was supposed to be hyping up our opponents. The rhythm was out of this world. *Man, I wanna play on this team.* When I heard my thoughts, I kind of shook my head to bring me back to the reality of the moment. As the song finished, their crowd erupted in a deafening cheer. The band had done their job. Their team was ready.

Favor was on their side.

But on that day, Pittsburg was no match for us. I had one of the best games of my high school career. I had three rushing touchdowns, assisted on two more, and played both sides of the ball. My teammates were incredible too. We played better together on that day than we had in any of our previous games.

After our victory, we had to have a police escort out of the neighborhood where their high school stadium was because of the heavy gang violence.

The game at Pittsburg set me on track for my breakout season.

My junior year was all about victories. I was winning on the field and off it as well.

I was already getting letters from colleges, but it wasn't until my junior year finished that I started believing I might actually go somewhere. Before, they had all been typed letters that were too general to really be talking to me, and they felt cold in nature. But as I got ready to go into my senior season, the letters shifted into handwritten letters. Their written words were unique to me and my skills. It was like I was getting the opportunity to sit down across from each coach and have an intimate conversation. There weren't as many handwritten ones as there were the other kind, but those were the ones I really started paying attention to.

"Hey, Mom, guess what? I got a letter today."

"Babe, you get letters every day."

"Not like this one. This one is handwritten."

Mom was as surprised as I was that a coach had taken the time to write to me personally. I finally began to believe that these letters might actually be the hand up I had been hoping for. Mom had taught us to never be looking for a handout but to work hard for all we got. I was definitely working hard and knew that these handwritten letters were serious.

As a kid, I honestly never envisioned myself playing football in college and definitely never thought a career in my favorite sport was even remotely imaginable. But when the letters started my sophomore year, even when they were still just typed and generic, I started to realize that life outside of Union City might really be possible.

"It's possible, Roy," Mom reminded me often.

I had to accept it and then develop the ability to believe in myself.

CHAPTER 5
WHATEVER IT TAKES

"**C**heck check check! Sixteen! Sixteen!"

I had finally made it to my senior year. Everything seemed like it was coming together. My whole career looked like it might be laying itself out in front of me. I was finally free from the bondage of dyslexia. The stars were aligned, and I just knew that everything was going to work out. Building on my success as a junior was going to be fun.

Early in the year, we were at practice in the afternoon just like we always were. It was a Tuesday, the practice of the week when we wore only helmets with a T-shirt and shorts but no pads. On that particular day, Coach had us doing a drill on tackling bags. Without pads on, a tackling bag can be rough on your shoulders. Technically, in a drill it's not so much about force as it is about form and technique. But I don't know how to go slow at anything, so I was hitting that bag all out.

All the while, Coach was screaming at us to go harder.

"C'mon, boys!"

"That's it, that's it!"

"You've got more than that!"

Coach was relentless. He was an expert in pushing us past our limits, which is a good thing if you're outfitted right for the task at hand. But we weren't.

I wanted so badly to respond to his pushing. I did in my mind. *We don't have any fuckin' pads on! C'mon, man! This is bullshit!* But I didn't say it out loud, and he didn't hear my thoughts.

My AC joint in my shoulder paid the price for his ridiculous requirements. Walking back into the locker room after practice, I could feel the pain deep inside my shoulder. Throbbing. A thousand needles stabbing me from the inside out.

I didn't go to the doctor, and I didn't tell anyone. Just like when I couldn't understand my first-grade teacher and said nothing, my shoulder was messed up now, and I kept quiet all over again.

Never missing a game, I continued to play as hard as I could. But I knew that my injury was holding me back. This was my senior season. I needed it to be my best season, but I felt like I was playing at half my capability.

A couple of weeks later, we were in the locker room watching a film. My shoulder had finally healed for the most part, and I felt like this next game, I was finally going to be able to play at full power. We were planning for me to play quarterback in the upcoming game. There were two quarterbacks on our team, and occasionally I would catch wind of some political mumbo jumbo about who should play, but at least for this game, I had won out.

Coach paused the film and leaned over toward me, poised to speak.

"Roy, we're going to put in a new play. It's gonna be a quarterback sneak."

He explained that when I got up to the line, if I could see that the defense was in a favorable formation for a quarterback sneak, all I would have to do was give the secret code.

"Check check check! Sixteen! Sixteen!" Coach modeled. "It will be especially helpful when we're in a goal line situation or just needing a couple of yards."

That would be the audible to alert the offensive line that there was going to be a sneak, so they could block accordingly.

Later that day, we were out on the field practicing against the

JV defensive unit. They never stood a chance. Their guys were so puny and weak compared to our O-line. In fact, their presence on the field was usually just a formality so that our offense would actually run the play instead of only going through the motions.

Coach had us running goal line drills. JV was taking a pounding.

We broke from the huddle, making our way to the line.

"Hey, Roy!"

I turned my head to the sideline. Sometimes Coach would call an audible from there with a set of signals that he had taught the quarterbacks. But he wasn't showing a signal. Instead, he was winking.

When I didn't get what he was trying to tell me, he said, "Hey, do the thing we talked about."

Since we were set up in a goal line drill, our job was to score. The junior varsity team was charged by the coaches to do whatever it took to keep us from scoring. It was a lopsided battle at best, but with their pride on the line, the JV always gave their best effort.

Under center, I scanned the defense.

"Check check check! Sixteen! Sixteen!"

I scanned one more time.

"Hike!"

My center snapped the ball just like he normally would, but when I started to make my move, the O-line stood up, but no one blocked. One of the JV D linemen saw his opportunity and shot through the gap. I tried to juke, but he had already wrapped me up. Spinning, I tried to break free, but my ankle got stuck in his grasp. That was when I heard it.

Snap!

It was my ankle. I knew it immediately. When I got just past center, I could feel it and hear it at the same time.

Pain immediately shot through me.

"Shit!"

I hate making a big deal over my pain. In fact, I would much rather no one know I'm hurting at all. But when my ankle snapped internally, my reaction shot out of my mouth like a rocket.

As I limped off the field with the help of our team trainer, my stare was blank and initially aimed at my offensive line. I felt like someone had set me up.

High ankle sprains are the worst. They can take forever to heal.

But at that moment, I wasn't even thinking about healing. I just wanted to limp off the field. My ankle was throbbing, and with watery eyes, I was trying to focus on my injury without cussing someone out. When I got up to walk off the field, not wanting any assistance from the trainers, I heard Coach call for the same play. Listening over my shoulder, I became consciously aware that they were still running the same drill.

Turning around ever so gently, so as not to tweak my ankle any more than it already had been, I attentively listened in as the other quarterback called the same audible.

"Check check check! Sixteen! Sixteen!"

"Hike!"

At the snap, I watched as my O-line, who had left me hanging out to dry, blew up the JV defense like they were just a bunch of little kids.

It was then that I understood what was happening. It wasn't my O-line at all who was at fault—no one told them what to do with the audible call. I had just assumed that Coach had told them about the call before I made it. But he didn't.

It felt wrong. Like he set me up, but I didn't know why.

The worst part was that I began to play mind games with myself about what went down. *Did Coach do that on purpose? I didn't ask for this. I just want to play football and have fun. Was he trying to get me hurt?*

The problem with those kinds of mind battles is you usually lose as soon as you start. But feeling like my coach had set me up set me back a bit. I played through the high ankle sprain even though the trainer suggested that I stay off it, but it was a fight against the injury every game.

Mom and Dad did not raise me to talk back to my elders, and that included coaches. But there were a couple of times during my senior year that I wish I could've said something.

Don't get me wrong, I had mad love and respect for our head coach at James Logan High School in Union City. For the most part, Coach Fromson led our team well and honored each of us and the talents that we brought to the team. But sometimes it's the little things.

If I had been wiser or more mature, or even a little braver, I would have gone to him with the intention of standing up for myself in a respectful way. But I wasn't those things, and I honestly didn't know how I could even bring it up without disrespecting my "elders." So I just kept quiet.

Halfway through my senior season, we had a game against Palo Alto High. I hadn't ever played against them in my career, so I wasn't quite sure what to expect. They were good, but you just never know what you're up against until you get on the field.

We lost the coin toss, and they chose to receive. But they didn't have the ball for long because I came up with an interception and moved 35 yards back into a great position to start our first drive.

Despite my ankle injury, I had won back the quarterback starting position. On our first offensive possession, I went under center with the intention of marching us down the field for 6 points.

"Hike!"

Just out of my peripheral vision, the defensive end came rushing around the corner, and for some reason my O-line didn't block him, giving him a clean shot on my blind side. Luckily, I saw him just before he came crashing into me and was able to roll my shoulders, flipping him off me. With the weak side now open, I tucked the ball, spun 360 degrees, and ran for it.

"First down!"

Back under center, my mind was previewing the deep crossing pattern that my strong-side wideout would be running. I knew if I could stay in the pocket long enough, he would be open. Palo Alto had already shown us that their secondary was weak.

"Twenty-three! Twenty-three! Hike!"

The defense called the same blitz pattern, and for some reason, my guy didn't block again. But this time, I didn't see him.

Pop!

In my high school career, I put some pretty powerful hits on people. And I've been hit really hard a couple of times too. The hit that defensive end put on me is one that I would rank up there on the high side of the list. He drove me downward, shoving my shoulder into the ground.

"Ahhh!"

My face twisted all up. No one saw me because my face mask was in the turf, but I could feel the pain shooting all throughout my upper back and down my arm. The hit reactivated my shoulder injury from earlier in the year.

Trainers came trotting onto the field almost as soon as they heard me shout in agony. After they carefully rolled me over, it took only one look.

"You're gonna have to come out, probably for the whole game."

Furious, I jumped up and ran off the field with my arm dangling. We lost.

Then the next week came. The coaches wanted me to play. I had a way of making things happen. If I couldn't play, I couldn't score.

"Listen, you can't play quarterback. But maybe receiver."

I didn't get to start on offense for a couple of games because my shoulder was really limiting my ability to extend my arm to make a catch. Instead, I spent all of my time playing cornerback on our defensive unit. I played hurt my whole year. If it wasn't my ankle, it was my shoulder.

Back when I first made varsity, Mom had warned me: "Don't get hurt."

Even though I was clearly injured and playing through it anyway, her support never waned. Uncle Leander and all his family were there at lots of games too. Sometimes my mom's sister, Aunt V, came also.

My dad would almost always come to my games, but he left early to go to this Friday night bowling league. He didn't know that I was injured because I didn't tell him. And because he never asked.

Fortunately, the interest from colleges didn't stop. In fact, on somewhat of a regular basis, the local sports reporters would come to my games. One of them found my dad at a game and interviewed him.

They asked him why I wasn't playing offense.

"Yeah, my son has bad ankles."

When I found out what he had said, I was pissed and confused. All that had gone down with Coach and my ankle came flooding back. All I wanted to do was give Dad a piece of my mind. *No, I don't. You don't even know 'cause you never talk to me. You're just making assumptions so that you don't look stupid in front of the reporter. Freakin' ridiculous!*

We were lucky that none of the colleges took him seriously. His statement could've ruined my career before it ever started. I didn't have bad ankles. I just had a coach who made a bad decision or a bonehead move by forgetting to tell the O-line about the secret code.

"Whatever it takes" never meant "whatever you feel like" or "whatever you want." It's balls to the wall 24-7.

But if I'm honest, the mind games played hard against me. Dad was saying stuff, Coach was making decisions that I didn't understand, and constantly fighting injuries made me wonder.

Am I good enough? Really?

It wasn't just about football either. This was my future.

CHAPTER 6
HARD WORK

B ack when I was just a freshman, before I made varsity, my Uncle Leander (Mom's brother) and I were having a conversation one day. In a lot of ways, he was my stand-in dad. Sometimes a boy just needs a man's words.

"Roy Lee"—that's what my family always called me when I was younger—"you've gotta consider other sports, like track or basketball, and how they will help you to better develop your game in football."

He hadn't steered me wrong before. So I went out for track.

I had ruled my own little Pop-Warner kingdom, but especially after my talk with my uncle, I didn't know if my rule could be the same as I entered high school. I honestly thought I was fast enough. But standing on the track for the first time, surrounded by runners of all shapes and sizes, I had questions rolling in my mind. *Am I really fast enough? What if I could be faster? More explosive? More powerful? Then what?*

There was a guy at my school named Pierre. In a roundabout way, he was like my cousin, even though he wasn't blood-related.

Whenever we got together as a family for holidays or barbeques, everybody came. Even though Pierre and I weren't related, at least not really, he came to most of those barbeques. So we used to hang out when we were younger.

But now, Pierre was my teammate, my inspiration, and my arch-nemesis. He was a young Usain Bolt, destined to be a record holder. At that moment, I was not. It took only one race between us to convince me that I had a lot of hard work to put in. If I wanted to improve my performance, then I was going to have to put my nose to the grindstone and work for it.

Thinking through my journey with football, I remembered back to when I knew very little about the game that quickly became my favorite thing in the world to do. Before jerseys and pads, even before playing with Lloyd Greenwood, I had to learn the little things.

When I ran the 40-yard dash as a freshman, it was embarrassing. A 5.4 40 was beyond slow.

I needed to work on my explosiveness. Part of me just wanted to race Pierre, but I knew then that I couldn't beat him. At least, not yet. So I tried out only for the jumping events like long jump and triple jump. The entire spring after my ninth-grade year of playing on the freshman football team, I trained my muscles to react quicker and to explode, carrying me farther.

No matter where I went, I was constantly skipping, jumping, and hopping. I measured my steps all the time.

When my sophomore year came, I could jump. I touched the rim at Coach's request, made varsity, and started making an impact on the team. But my speed still wasn't what I wanted it to be. Was I faster than a lot of my teammates? Sure. But I knew that outside of my little bubble, there were guys who were faster.

So, when track season came around again, I signed up for the sprints. I ran the 100, 200, and 4 x 100 relay. At the beginning of that season, my track coach called me out.

"Roy, I know if you work at this, you *can* run faster."

So, I worked, and I worked, and I worked. That year I ran a 4.8 40. Finally, late in the season, I lined up against Pierre and five or six other guys in the 200-meter dash. But as far as I was concerned, this race was a one-on-one match race.

All the runners stretched, shook their legs out, and one by one got down into their starting positions.

When the starter official was in place, I zoned everything out.

"On your marks."

"Get set."

Then, just like with every other race before and after it, I began a conversation with myself in my head.

Dude, Pierre is going to get out quick. So I have to get out quick. Pow!

The sound of the starter's gun interrupted my thoughts.

I burst out of my starting blocks. *Go, just go!* I shouted internally. *Don't even worry about looking around. Stay with him. Lean into the turn! Lean into it!*

From the outside looking in, Pierre and I were all alone, in stride with one another. There was no one else in the heat who would be a contender. But I wasn't worried about anyone else. All I wanted to do was run my own race. And beat Pierre, but I couldn't think about that now.

Now remember, Roy, whatever you do ... wait till you hit that mark.

When I practiced, I had made a mental note of a certain mark on the track where I would start my kick. It was of the utmost importance that I spent enough effort to get either in-stride or slightly in front of him, but it was also equally important that I saved enough effort so that I would have some left for the last part of the race.

Just wait till you hit that mark, and kick in your rocket booster.

When I saw the mark in the track, I did just what I had told myself to do. I stepped on my gas pedal a little bit harder. The feeling as I floated down the straightaway was truly surreal.

Don't look back. Just put your head down and run!

I leaned into the finish, and as I trotted to a walk, I finally realized that I had beaten him.

It was a sweet victory. He ate my dust.

Winning against Pierre was a real game changer for me. He had been the unbeatable runner, my inspiration to work extra hard, and in a lot of ways, my idol who I had always looked up to. But when I beat him, I felt so empowered.

Gradually, people began to notice my growth.

"Good job, Roy!"

"Way to go, Roy!"

"We're rootin' for you!"

It seemed like every time I finished a race or a field event, my track coach was right there to praise me for my hard work. If it wasn't him, it would be a voice from the stands or one of my teammates.

The more I heard these voices of affirmation, the more I worked. I don't like to brag, and I despise people who try to make themselves out to be a bigger deal than everyone else. But in my life, I avoided bragging so much that I began to believe the opposite about my own skills and talents. Coach's encouragement began to reverse that for me. The more I worked, the more I realized that his words were true until I really believed them. My self-worth skyrocketed.

When track started my junior year, I had just finished my best season yet on the football field. I signed up for sprints again. Now, I wanted to beat Pierre not only once but every time. For the most part, that is just what I did. I improved my time again when I ran a 4.6 40. The roles were reversed. Pierre was chasing me now. And now I wasn't chasing anyone. I knew I wasn't the fastest guy out there, but I was beating the guy who used to blow me away.

My passion for football was always the drive behind my

involvement in other sports. I didn't join the basketball team at school because sometimes the football and basketball seasons overlapped, but I played pickup games all the time in my neighborhood.

The blood, the sweat, and the tears were all finally proving to be worth it.

I had worked so hard for so long.

Because of the work that I had done with Miss Judy, Miss Taylor, and Ms. B, I was going to graduate on my own merit. I had finally felt ready during the football season to take the ACT a second time, and to my delight, I was successful.

I passed.

I remembered back to the days when football was simple. No jersey, no pads, no coaches (except the self-appointed ones like Imoni), no recruiters, just all-out, go-hard-every-minute, full-contact, knock-you-on-your-ass football.

As I got lost in my silent mind space, a powerful thought suddenly blew up in my mind.

This might really be possible. If I'm getting recruited to play at the college level, what if that means that I can play professionally as well? What if ... maybe ... I can play for my team, America's team, the Dallas Cowboys.

It was then that I noticed that something began to change in my attitude. Before, when I believed that I was just an illiterate, dumb, disruptive idiot, I could never see a favorable future. But now I could see my own potential. I've never been big on bragging, but learning how to tell myself the truth about who I was and what I was becoming was a monumental shift.

A lot of people still viewed me as the old me. But now I didn't care as much.

One of the kids who worked on the yearbook asked if she

could ask me a question and that my answer could be printed in the final product.

"Where do you see yourself in four years?"

I never hesitated. "I'll be playing for the Dallas Cowboys."

After all that I had accomplished, I really believed that it could come true.

Slowly throughout my high school years, I began to recognize how much of my life I had learned within the boundaries of the 100 yards. And I wasn't even half-grown yet.

When I realized that my teachers deserved the same respect that I gave to my coaches, things in the classroom really began to turn around.

My work ethic predated the high school field, but it was definitely something that formed in my budding love for the game.

Tenacity and perseverance were skills that were minted on the field.

Most of all, the rough-and-tumble produced a don't-give-up and don't-give-in attitude that was built in between the hash marks—chalked and not.

CHAPTER 7
READY

This was the end. High school was almost over.

Passing the ACT gave me the confidence to finally visit some of the universities that I was considering.

Sometimes after school, you could find me just sitting on my bed holding a handful of recruiting letters. They all had so many nice things to say about me, and I would just sit there soaking in their words of affirmation. It was strange ... the narrative changed so much in a very short amount of time. I went from being the disruptive knucklehead that no teacher wanted in their class to the guy who was getting invitations right and left from every college under the sun, and all of them wanted me at their university.

I shuffled the letters like a deck of cards, looking only at the header on each one. As I went through them, I began to internally read the names of each school.

UCLA ... USC ... Notre Dame ... Nebraska ...

Fresno State.

I chuckled out loud, thinking about how mad I had been when the Fresno State head coach had told me I could come there *if I couldn't pass* the ACT. But I was also grateful in a way that he had said it like that because his statement really lit a fire under me to work even harder to pass.

Oregon ... Cal Berkeley ...

Utah ...BYU ... Boise State ... Oregon State ... Washington State ...

I breathed deeply and then let it all out.

Putting the letters back in the shoebox, I had already settled in my mind where I thought I would go. Part of me really wanted to get out of California, but I wasn't sure that was the right decision. I thought I was going to go to UCLA.

So we planned a visit and went to see the university and check out the Bruins facility. Bob Toledo was the head coach, and he seemed like a good guy to play for. I had received typed and hand-written letters as well as a couple of phone calls from UCLA, so they were definitely a real contender.

When we parked the car on campus that day, Mom and I were taken aback at how beautiful the campus was. It was immaculate.

The temperature was just right, a beautiful blue sky rose above us, and the sun was shining. Plus, there was a ton of eye candy all over campus, beautiful ladies as far as the eye could see.

Right away, I met Deshawn Foster. He was getting recruited at the same time as I was, and we hit it off. The university had us paired up that day with wide receiver Freddie Mitchell. And I honestly was having a great time with the two of them before we ever even started the tour.

"Honey ..." Mom almost had to shout to get a word in.

Deshawn and I were already cutting up with each other like we'd been friends for years.

"Roy! Hey, do you like it here?"

She could already sense there was something about this place that was clicking with me.

"Yeah, I like it, but we haven't seen anything yet."

Freddie motioned with his hand, beckoning us all to follow. "We'll start today at the track."

I would have said that it looked like any normal track, except this one featured a very unique personality. We couldn't believe it.

It was Bill Cosby! Running around the track, minding his own business.

"Man, I'm coming to UCLA!" The words popped out of my mouth before I could stop them.

I was sold on becoming a Bruin at that moment.

There were other benefits too: They had a great program, I liked Bob Toledo, and even more importantly, I got along with the guys, like Freddie and Deshawn. I knew that they would be like my brothers for four years.

Our trip home that day was joyful—it's always enjoyable traveling with Mom. I felt like I had pretty much made my decision. But we decided to think about it. Still, Damian had accepted an offer to play at Stanford University. So, if I went to UCLA, then I could be just a day's drive from hanging out with my boy.

We still had football to play at home. Our team was bound for the championship game. It did not go like we had hoped. Damian had to be carted off in the third quarter because he tore his knee up pretty badly.

On the Saturday morning after my final high school football game, I woke up without an alarm. We had just played for the big one, but much to our disappointment, we lost.

I couldn't sleep, and I had gotten up earlier than I wanted to. All the years of work and play were jumbled in my head. I sat down on the edge of the bed, pondering in silence.

In the midst of the quiet, I began to look forward to the future. My future.

Losing the championship game in my senior year was not what I wanted. It isn't what I thought the prospective colleges would want either.

Stanford had just notified Damian that they were going to have to withdraw his scholarship and offer. Since he had hurt his knee, they didn't feel like he would ever fully recover.

I sure didn't want losing the championship to be the reason that I lost my offers. Then we'd both be shit out of luck.

I called Bob Toledo to tell him about my dilemma.

"Coach, I thought I knew. You've offered me a chance, but now I'm questioning."

He gave me some surprising but great advice.

"Listen, Roy. Go ahead and go on your other visits."

"Really?"

"Sure, you've gotta make the best decision for you. Go enjoy the process."

If he hadn't shared that with me, I would have felt obligated to go with the offer from UCLA. No player in my position knows exactly what they're doing. There wasn't anyone holding my hand through the recruiting process, and it can sometimes be pretty complicated.

So I did as he suggested.

Next, I went to visit Cal Berkeley. It was cool for what it was, but it just wasn't my jam. Honestly, it felt a bit stuffy. I learned very quickly that Cal has a very high regard for educational excellence, and I had just learned how to read. I just didn't fit. Plus, it was way too close to home, only fifteen or twenty minutes, and I really wanted some space in between where I grew up and my next step.

When we got home from Cal, things were quiet for a few weeks. But what I didn't know was that my Aunt V was working for us. She had a job in the athletic cafeteria at the University of Oklahoma at the time. She tracked down Steve Owens, who was the athletic director back in the day, and told him about me and Damian.

"I'd sure appreciate it if you would check them out. They would really like to come to OU."

Even though I'm sure an iconic AD like Steve probably got

approached by every college faculty member about their son or nephew, my aunt was successful in at least starting the process.

After months of trying to heal, my shoulder and my ankle were finally as good as new. Track season had officially started.

By that time, we had already sent film to OU for them to watch, and they in turn had begun sending us handwritten letters. Lots of handwritten letters.

One day at track practice, Damian and I were cutting up while we were stretching.

"Hey, guys, who the hell is that?"

One of our teammates interrupted our jokes to point out a short-statured White guy dressed as a cowboy who was walking across the track, headed in our direction. He had on a black cowboy hat, a black collared shirt, black starched jeans, black boots, and a black leather coat. The only thing that wasn't black was his belt buckle. It was a huge shiny silver buckle that flashed in the California sun.

Before the guy was in earshot, Damian joked, "Who is this country mofo right here?"

"Hi, young men. I'm Coach Joe Dickerson, the offensive coordinator for the University of Oklahoma."

We shook his hand and tried not to look too surprised that he had flown all the way from Oklahoma to pay the two of us a visit.

But secretly, we were more than surprised. We were shocked.

He didn't let on that he noticed our raised eyebrows. Instead, he just kept the conversation going.

"Based on the stories that your aunt has been sharing with us, it sounds like you two are interested in Oklahoma." His tone rose at the end, signifying his statement as a question.

"Yeah," we responded in unison.

Later that evening, he visited both of our homes to sit down with us and our parents to talk about the details.

At 4212 Solar Circle, with only my mom, I made sure Coach Joe knew that the only way I was going to really consider coming to Oklahoma was if Damian was coming too.

"We're a package deal."

I never talked about that in front of Damian, even though I don't think he would have cared. But had the roles been reversed and I had been the one with the torn-up knee, he would've done the same for me.

A week or two later, we flew to Oklahoma to visit the campus to meet with head coach John Blake.

We met with him one at a time, while the other got to see the entire facility.

Walking into his office on the southwest end of the stadium was like walking into the president's office. He had the two Super Bowl rings that he had won with the Dallas Cowboys, as well as some other things that looked impressive.

"Have a seat." His voice boomed in the quiet of his office.

"So, are you gonna come to OU? Help us build our defense so we can win a National Championship?"

"Listen, Coach, I'll come." I paused for just a second—Mom always said I was a born negotiator. "But if you want me, you're gonna have to give my boy, Damian, a scholarship too."

He never even hesitated.

"Oh yeah, we're gonna offer him a scholarship."

"Well, alright then, I'll come."

And they did. They offered us both scholarships on that same day. But for whatever reason, we didn't sign that day.

With our visit over and offers on the table, we flew home.

I never quite knew where my dad's head was at. He wasn't

home when Coach Dickerson visited the house, and I'm not sure he even knew that the visit had taken place. He thought I was going to UCLA. But when he found out that I was considering moving halfway across the country, he was shocked and disappointed.

I had scheduled one last visit to Washington State, but after my trip to OU went so well, I didn't want to go, and I told my mom. My mind was already made up that I was going to Oklahoma.

I was pumped. Not only was my school choice made, but now I was going to be free to go with my Uncle Leander on his annual ski trip. I had gone with him the year before and had a blast.

After dinner one evening, my mom broke the news to Dad about my decision. I got up from the table and headed toward the stairs. Even though I was seventeen, I still didn't have an understanding of how much a plane ticket costs or what my mom was willing to lose on the basis of my decision to not go to Washington.

"Roy!" My dad followed me to the stairs, intent on having a conversation with me.

He wanted me to visit Washington State, but looking over my shoulder as I walked away, I straight up told him no.

Grabbing my shoulders, he spun me 180 degrees so I would face him. In a rage, he grabbed my shirt and picked me up, slamming me against the corner of the wall. I could feel the picture frames stabbing into my back like dull-pointed knives.

"You're fuckin' going to Washington State! Your mom paid good money for the plane ticket."

So, against my wishes, I went on a visit to Washington State to appease my father.

It was freakin' cold the whole time we were there! I'm a Northern California boy through and through, so I was not prepared for ice and snow all over the road and me. I was miserable.

Thankfully, the visit was quick, and the plane was able to take off despite the weather.

A week later, Damian came over to my house to play video games. We were sitting on the couch when he leaned forward with something on his mind.

"Hey, dude, so are we gonna go to OU or not?"

"I don't care." I smiled because I knew he was just prodding me. "Man, I got options. I mean, do you wanna go?"

"Yeah, I think we can make that work." He chuckled.

"OK, let's go to OU."

There was no fanfare or press conference when we signed on the dotted line. We got together and signed our letters of intent at my mom's house while we both sat on the couch. Nothing fancy, just two guys who loved to play football.

Track season brought mixed emotions. It would be the last sport I would participate in at James Logan High, but knowing that OU was definitely on my horizon made everything just great.

I was excited to compete in my events, especially since I was fully recovered from all of my injuries. Beating Pierre would make me feel even better after my senior football season, which had been one injury and inconvenience after another. I ran the sprints just like I had in my sophomore and junior seasons. My improvement in the 40-yard dash was staggering. I had moved my time from a super slow 5.4 to a 4.47 in just four years. Now I was ready for college ball.

Uncle Leander had been right. Playing multiple sports had enhanced my abilities in a different way than if I had just played one. My investment in time and hard work had paid off.

I was ready for the University of Oklahoma before I ever walked across the stage to receive my high school diploma.

But I did walk across the stage. For most, this is a small feat, but for me it was monumental. I don't know whose smile was bigger on that day, mine or Mom's. I couldn't have done without her or Miss Judy, Miss Taylor, and Ms. B. They believed in me before I had proven myself.

With my diploma in hand, I made my way back to my seat among my classmates. On my way down the aisle, I made eye contact with Mom and read her lips.

"Way to go, son!"

Now I was ready for college.

Uncle
Leander

CHAPTER 8
SUPERMAN

"P lease take a seat."

The professor's voice echoed in the cavern of a classroom as I entered at the back, looking down the stairs where she stood speaking as we came through the main door. Her hair was gray, her woman's business suit was monotone, and her voice sent chills down my spine, me knowing that I was stuck here for an entire semester trying to learn while listening to that voice. This was not at all what I was used to. It was more like the Colosseum than a classroom. There must have been five hundred of us in English 101.

When we had all done as she instructed, I very quickly realized that I might be in very big trouble. She spoke so quickly and wrote on the board even quicker. Plus, the board was like a mile away and nearly impossible to see from my seat.

I can't even figure out what she's saying, much less understand it. My mind was whirling.

There was a stark reminder hanging in the air that I no longer had a Ms. B waiting down the hall. There was no one I could go see after class to help me translate all the things that this teacher had just spewed out all over me.

The lecture setting was extremely intimidating. On the outside I was trying to remain calm, but on the inside, I was freaking out a little bit. I'd never seen anything like this in my life. I tried to take notes as fast as I could, but the professor used so many unfamiliar words that I was lost within minutes.

Thankfully, the university provided help, not just for athletes but for students like me with disabilities such as dyslexia. I was able to get a notetaker who sat in class with me and took all the notes, so I could just focus and listen. The greatest thing about the help was that the university made it possible for me to feel like I was just like everyone else. When it comes to disabilities, sometimes all you want is to be seen as normal.

I ended up redshirting in my first year on the football field. I still went to workouts and practiced like everyone else, but it also gave me an opportunity to get acclimated to college as a whole. By the end of my first year, I surprised everyone, including myself, when I made the honor roll.

School was finally going well for me, but at the end of that year, John Blake got fired from the head coaching position, and my football career felt like it hung in the balance of the unknown future. I wasn't the only one: A lot of the guys on the team were concerned too. We were without a coach for nearly four months. There was Coach Johnson, but he let us get away with way too much. Gradually, our midsections grew larger, and our muscles grew smaller. I should've known better, but when the older guys sloughed off, so did I. No practice didn't mean don't practice, but that's the way we interpreted it.

At the beginning of 1999, OU hired Coach Bob Stoops. Let's just say that we didn't put our best foot forward at our first practice with our new coach and his staff. We were fat and out of shape. But that's where our new strength and conditioning coach, Jerry Schmidt, came in. Fat and out of shape was his specialty, or at least, that's what we all thought after our first workout.

"Alright, boys, let's put in the work!"

Coach Schmidt didn't joke around. He was all business.

It was six o'clock in the morning, and the whole team was gathered as we had been instructed at the indoor track.

He got us started right away. We were exhausted almost immediately. There was faint chatter between the guys, but we made sure our voices were hushed so as not to be heard.

"This is kinda hard."

"C'mon, guys, we got this."

"I can't keep this up."

"Yeah, you can. C'mon."

I guess that Coach Schmidt could have heard us, but he never let on, and we weren't about to let him know that it was as hard as it was. But it wouldn't have taken a brain surgeon to figure out that we were out of shape and in need of some assistance.

Honestly, it was the first difficult workout I'd had since I left James Logan. Workouts last year with Coach Blake just weren't that hard.

"Alright, guys, circle up." Waving his hands toward all of us, he called us to the center of the facility.

Following Coach Schmidt's direction, we began to clap in a syncopated rhythm together.

Clap. Clap. Clap.

Clap. Clap. Clap.

"Alright, you guys. That was a good warm-up."

You could hear a gasp escape from more than one mouth, like air escapes a tire, except this was all at once.

"Now we're about to get it in today's workout."

He wasn't kidding either. He didn't kid ever. Heads shaking. Hands on hips. Bodies bent in half. Heavy breathing. We were so defeated at that point.

"Are you freakin' serious?" One of the guys let his thoughts of desperation slip out of his mouth, but Coach Schmitt didn't even bat an eye.

After that day and for the next several days, you could see the worry on the faces of coaches and players alike. We were all wondering the same thing: Does this team have what it takes?

The '99 season was a battle of love and hate and figuring out how to get along while getting to know one another all at the same time.

Coach Mike Stoops was a lifesaver to me.

"Roy, anytime you need something, my door is always open."

I didn't start in the first part of the '99 season. I just played special teams and occasional special packages or different defensive schemes. What I did do was spend as much time as I possibly could with Coach Mike Stoops. I wanted to know the defense, but I needed help. He spent hours working with me so that I would understand exactly what everything was and what my job was on each play. Midseason, I finally broke into the starting line-up.

Every athlete who has ever run out when your name and number are being called knows the high that it gives you right before the game starts. Once I had heard it, I never gave up my starting position.

That year we started out as a team at 3–0, scoring 40-plus points in all three of our first games. We were surprising everyone, including ourselves. Then we traveled to South Bend, Indiana, to play Notre Dame. We were winning in the first half, up by 9. But when the Irish came out to start the second half, they took the upper hand.

We lost 30–34.

Seven days later, I found myself in the tunnel at the Cotton Bowl for the Red River Shootout against our arch-nemesis, Texas. The tension in that tunnel just before we made our appearance on the field was so thick. I didn't grow up as an Oklahoma fan, but there is almost an instantaneous hatred for that burnt orange color that is developed in you as soon as you put on the crimson and cream.

"You're goin' down!"

"Shit! We'll see."

The banter back and forth between us and them started way before we ever stepped past the white lines and onto the field. Hatred and adrenaline mixed together like nitroglycerin and sodium nitrate. It's never a question of will the dynamite go off, but when.

The coin was tossed, and the kickoff flew. As the ball sailed downfield, on the sideline you could almost hear some of the guys remembering how badly they crushed us last year. 34–3 was not an impressive stand—in fact, it was downright embarrassing.

But this was a new year. In that first quarter, we jumped out to an early lead. Josh Heupel was leading our offense, and they looked good. When the Texas offensive unit came trotting onto the field, I saw Major Applewhite for the first time. When I saw him, I thought, *Who the hell is this skinny little White guy?* In the first quarter, he just didn't match up with us. We kept them guessing, and our defense held the Longhorns to a measly 3 points. Going into the second quarter, we felt good. But that didn't last for long.

We were up by 14.

I still don't quite understand what happened to Major Applewhite in between the first and second quarter, but when he came out for our second fifteen minutes, he was a totally different opponent. My opinion of him quickly changed. He was a baller and an incredible athlete.

They scored 14. Sure, we made some key stops on defense, but our offense just couldn't get anything going, leaving us scoreless. At halftime, we were tied.

I don't remember what Coach Stoops said to us in the locker room. We went back out ready for battle and made some forward progress. But Applewhite and company were too much for us.

Final score: 38–28, Texas.

There is just one tunnel at the Cotton Bowl because both locker rooms are at the same end of the field. When the game ended and we started up the tunnel, we were on one side, and they were on the other. Trash talk went flying like artillery shells from side to side. Applewhite was leading the way.

"Ya'll are a joke!"

"Just couldn't hack it today, could ya?"

I was disappointed. Angry. Frustrated. We had been winning. But we just couldn't seal the deal. I wanted to punch him in his pretty little mouth. Instead, I made a very loud internal promise to myself.

No matter what it takes, I will never lose to Texas again. No matter what I have to do, no matter what is required of me, I will not lose to the Longhorns again!

It was a solemn bus ride home.

But thankfully, one loss wasn't enough to shut us down for the entire season.

Coach Schmidt's workouts put us back into position to really do something as a unit. Then Coach Bob Stoops took over from there. He ran a tight ship, and we were still adjusting to one another. But we all knew where we were going and who was driving.

After all was said and done, we finished the season with a 7–5 record. The biggest accomplishment for the program was that while doing it, we made our way to OU's first bowl game since 1994. We walked away with a tough loss to Ole Miss, but 1999 was a building season.

When the 2000 season rolled around, we were a totally

different team. But when the schedule was released, it was a big reality check. There was more than one conversation going on around campus between different players.

"Have you seen the schedule?"

"Yeah, we've got all these non-conference games against no-joke contenders."

"Then we've gotta play Texas, K-State, and Nebraska. Back to back to back."

"Man, this is gonna be tough!"

Things weren't just different on campus. There was a new excitement across what I had come to know as Sooner Nation. Everywhere you went on campus and in Norman, there was a buzz that this just might be a new team that was more like the glory days, instead of a team like the recent days.

But when Coach Stoops called our attention to the schedule, he never said anything about how difficult it was going to be. He talked only about how hard we were going to have to work.

When the BCS rankings came out, we were ranked No. 19. Coach Stoops never paid much attention to the ranking. But for us players, it was hard not to notice that the world of sports was finally seeing us for who we were becoming. No. 19 wasn't at the top, but at least it wasn't at the bottom either.

Still, our enemy across the Red River was ranked higher and expected to be the shoo-in for the Big 12 South title. In our second game of conference play, there was no sports analyst who thought OU was going to win the rivalry game against Texas.

As we ran through the tunnel at the Cotton Bowl for the annual Red River Shootout, I'm surprised that my teammates couldn't hear my thoughts as I almost screamed inside. Shaking with anticipation, I was reminding myself of the promise I had made last year.

No matter what it takes, I will never lose to Texas again!

My thoughts echoed inside of me, the hair on the back of my neck stood, and adrenaline coursed through my veins. I was ready.

Lucky for us, Coach Mike Stoops and Coach Venables had our defense well prepared for the Texas matchup. We were battle-tested, and our unit as a whole was ready for the gridiron war that was about to break out in Dallas.

In the opinion of most, it was too cold, rainy, and dreary of a day for football. But not for me. I like playing in the rain.

Since 1932 Oklahoma has worn their home-team crimson-top and white-pants uniform combo every even year when playing against Texas in the Cotton Bowl. The October 7, 2000, game was no exception. With over seventy-five thousand fans in attendance, we jogged onto the field as the home team.

Texas might have gone home with the win the last three years, but it was time for that streak to end. Our entire team agreed, and it seemed that the stars were aligned in our favor for just that exact thing to happen. Only no one knew it until we all knew it.

As we broke out of the dark shadows of the tunnel and onto the field, the anticipation from the fans could be physically felt.

The game that was about to play out in front of the crimson-and-burnt-orange fans would be one to remember for the ages.

Major Applewhite was there like last year, but even a playmaker like him couldn't make any difference in the inevitable result of that early October game. Texas had been indecisive leading up to the game about who their quarterback would be. Applewhite or Simms? We were determined to win no matter who took the snap.

By halftime, Heupel and company had scored 35, and our defense had scored 7 on Calmus's interception while only allowing Texas 7. Our total 42 points were just 2 points shy of what Texas had allowed in all of their previous games combined.

In our halftime meeting, Coach Stoops said nothing about slowing down. Even if he had, Texas's upset victory last year was still ringing in our ears, and we had no intention of letting up now.

The fans in attendance that represented Sooner Nation that day were absolutely coming unglued. We really were the home team on that day.

"Boomer!"

"Sooner!"

Their shouts were what continued to fuel us down the backstretch.

When the last quarter counted down, the scoreboard told the rest of the story.

63–14.

We did what Barry Switzer used to call "hung a half-a-hundred on 'em" and then some more.

It was a sweet, sweet victory! I'll never forget how quiet Texas was on their trot back up the tunnel on that day.

Even as sweet as it was, there was no parade waiting for us when we arrived home back in Oklahoma. In just seven days, we were set to face off against the No. 2-ranked Kansas State.

As we prepared all week, Coach Mike Stoops said only one thing to me on repeat.

"Jerrod Cooper is the best safety I've ever coached. You couldn't hold his jockstrap, Roy! You'll never play at his level."

Coach Bob, Coach Mike, and Coach Venables had come to OU from Kansas State, where they had worked under the legendary Coach Bill Snyder.

According to Coach Mike, this Cooper guy was legit and way more talented than I could ever be.

His taunting and reverse psychology was working. When game time came on Saturday, October 14, I was all set to have a good-ass game and show the fuck off. Then maybe I could prove Coach Mike wrong and change his mindset.

Running out onto the field, I was having another internal conversation. *Let's do this! I'm about to outshine Cooper's punk ass so much that Coach Mike won't have anything else to say.*

I knew going in that Coach Phil Bennett was the defensive coordinator for K-State. He had been a coach at OU when I first arrived in '98, under Coach John Blake. I've got a lot of love and respect for him, and I knew that he would be leading their defense to be hard-nosed.

After the coin was tossed, the game began. K-State had not lost in their last 25 at-home games. Everyone on our sideline knew that we were going to have to battle.

Our offense jumped out to an outstanding start. It was back and forth for sure, both teams wanting this one. But by halftime the score was telling a different story than what the BCS rankings showed.

"Touchdown Oklahoma!" The game announcer was mic'd up, like always, but he must have had to shout to be heard over the deafening noise coming from the fifty-three thousand-plus fans in attendance that day. With just 3:19 left in the first half, Griffin broke three tackles and ran for another six. After the extra point, we closed out the first half 31–14.

Even with our two-touchdown lead, in the locker room Coach Bob Stoops was very much all business.

"Listen, men, we cannot go into the second half and underestimate Coach Snyder and this Wildcat team."

I wanted this win badly. Uncle Leander was up in the stands watching. He was at every game, but I wanted this one.

As we started in on the second half, our lead of 17 was reminding us of what we were capable of when we played as a unit.

We received the kickoff to start the second half. On a short pass completion from Heupel, Antwone Savage ran for 74 yards and another touchdown. When I took the field for our first defensive sequence, I made eye contact with Coach Phil Bennett.

"Ya'll are losing today," I mouthed. The stadium was so loud, he couldn't have heard me even if I had shouted. But he understood because in response he moved his whole head toward the clock and then looked back at me.

"Game ain't over yet."

Reading his lips, I really hoped I wouldn't have to eat my words.

K-State got a field goal on that drive, but they weren't ranked No. 2 for no reason. In the first five minutes of the fourth quarter, they came to life in a powerful way. Their quarterback connected for a 69-yard touchdown, cutting the lead again. Then with 10:31 to play, their special teams came up big when they blocked one of our punts.

Whenever our offense is on fourth down, our defensive unit is always on the edge of the sideline because we know we've got to be prepared to go make our next stand.

We watched as Heupel got sacked on second and third down. Then we looked on as the Wildcat special teams broke through the line and blocked the punt.

"Get him!" someone from the sideline screamed.

But it was too late. They had already scored.

As I looked up at the sea of purple-dressed fans who seemed to be louder than ever, I saw something that day that I had never experienced before and have not seen since. I'm still not sure to this day if my eyes were watering or if I really saw what I thought was happening. The stadium was shaking.

Our lead was cut to just one touchdown, and I immediately

thought of Coach Phil Bennett. I could still see his lips form the words, "Game ain't over yet."

A teammate beside me spoke in exasperation: "Holy shit!"

The Wildcats kicked it out of the end zone, and then Heupel went to work, and we really had something going. But on a half-back option pass, K-State came up with a huge interception.

As the defense gathered, Coach Mike Stoops was clear.

"We gotta make a fuckin' play! Right here! Right now!"

First down and second down were unsuccessful for the Wildcats' offense. They attempted a screen play on third down, and I was able to bring down #5, Morgan, well short of the first down.

"C'mon!"

As Heupel and the guys jogged back onto the field, every guy in crimson was on his feet.

If it hadn't been for Josh Norman, I'm not sure we would have been able to convert on the first third down of that last drive. The offense fought hard and were able to cap off their drive with a field goal, extending our lead to 41–31.

As our defense made our way back onto the field, we knew it was our job to shut them down. With the last seconds ticking off on the clock, the game ended with a desperate throw toward the end zone that we intercepted.

Leaving Manhattan on that day, we felt like a different team. The world began to look at us like a different team too.

The only team that we felt could really stand in our way of making more out of our season was Nebraska.

Sportscasters from around the country started calling it Red October. We were just trying to focus on shifting our minds off Kansas State and onto No. 1-ranked Nebraska. Still, coming off the hard-fought battle in Manhattan didn't hurt us any, especially since we had come out on top.

The biggest difference was that for the first time in three weeks, we would be playing at home. It was expected that the full force of the Sooner Nation would be in attendance.

But even still, the implications of the upcoming game were huge! You didn't have to look very far to find a notable voice talking about what would happen for the winner of the OU–Nebraska game.

ABC Sports was covering the game, and I learned later that one of their analysts said, "Whoever wins this game will almost certainly play for the National Championship in the FedEx Orange Bowl."

When the first quarter kicked off, Nebraska didn't waste any time.

It was a shit show, at least at the beginning. We were prepared, maybe even overprepared. More than once, I completely overran that play. My teammates and I knew exactly what Nebraska's offense was going to be doing before they did it. But the problem was that we were playing so fast that we were getting to where they were going to be before them. As a consequence, we were missing tackles and letting them run past us.

Before the first quarter was even over, they had jumped out to a 14–0 lead.

Then just before the second quarter, Heupel put together an impressive drive but couldn't get it in the end zone.

On the sidelines, Coach Mike and Coach Venables gathered the defense.

"Everybody needs to calm the fuck down!"

"You guys are playing way too fast. Overrunning plays."

Looking around, I could see my teammates and I were in agreement, shaking our heads as our coaches charged us to go back out there and play the game our way.

We did as we were instructed. Settled in. Locked in on our targets and shut them down.

Finally, as we broke into the second quarter, our offense was able to put 7 points on the board.

Then, with 10:52 left in the half, we scored again.

When you live by the blitz like Nebraska does, sometimes when everything comes together just right for the offense, then you die by the blitz.

"Tie ball game, baby!"

The momentum shifted. Our defense went out on the field with the intention to continue to shut down Eric Crouch and company. We had down on about the 21-yard line as they prepared to punt.

"Blocked! The punt is blocked!" the announcer screamed through the microphone.

"It was Josh Norman lying out to block it."

The stadium erupted in earsplitting noise as Woolfolk fell on the ball on the 4-yard line.

The Huskers were able to keep us out of the end zone, but we walked away with another 3 points, taking the lead 17–14.

Nebraska didn't score again the rest of the game. Fans started throwing oranges onto the field in the fourth quarter. And we went on to win 31–14.

After successfully winning all three games in what has become the legendary Red October, the conversations about our program and our potential shifted drastically.

We were no longer the No. 19 team that started the season— now we were the No. 1 team expected to contend for the National Championship.

Instead of hearing wishful conversations of unseen hope

around campus, now you could hear the confidence that came with a 7–0 record.

"We could win this."

"Have you seen the Sooner's football team this year?"

"They look a bit like Switzer's team."

"Yeah, the Big 12 Championship is ours for the taking."

"We could win it all!"

The more guys I talked to, the more guys I realized were having the exact same conversations in their dorms or apartments, at lunch, or in the weight room. Trent Smith said it in his house. Frank Romero said almost the exact same thing with some of the other offensive linemen. We were in sync as a team, and our fan base was coming into alignment as we continued to give them reasons to believe in who we were and who we were becoming.

Coach Stoops never let up on us to be better every game. We kept winning. There were some close games, but all that we had to go through in '99 built us for what was coming in 2000.

In between games, I was still spending more time with Coach Mike. His door really was always open. I wanted to understand his terminology and why he was calling certain plays during different sets. He was tutoring me in football but even more so in life. I needed more time to process some things. But I was driven to understand why we did what we did and what I could do from my position to make it work better.

It could have been that he saw that I needed the extra help or that he saw an untapped potential in me, but whatever his reasons, he chose to make the investment in me every time I knocked on his office door.

Our conversations about the schedule were coming true. We had some stiff competition, but we were winning. In fact, we won every game that year. Our victories led us right to the

Big 12 Championship game against Kansas State, and we won again, 27–24.

That was when the oranges really started to rain from the stands onto the field. Now our fans weren't just hopeful that we might go to the Orange Bowl: we knew we were going.

After that, we didn't play for thirty-two days, which is a long time off in between games. But with Coach Stoops at the helm, we used it wisely. We were preparing for the championship that no one thought we could win.

Ready doesn't even come close to communicating how we all felt when our plane finally landed in Miami.

When Coach Bob Stoops came to OU in 1999, he taught us to be mentally prepared for every down. He had this business mentality about him that never allowed him to be too high or too low, but to always keep a level head about everything. Like a general, he trained us to never be too boastful or braggy about making plays because that could cause your head to become "unlevel" for the next play.

An ESPN reporter asked me what I thought prior to the National Championship game.

"We've been underestimated the whole season," I told them. "We're used to it. We're not worried about it. It's motivation."

On January 3, 2001, we gathered in the locker room at Pro Player Stadium for the National Championship game. Right before we went into the tunnel, Coach Stoops always had a few words for us.

"Men! We have one more game left. Today we have unfinished business. Now go out there and execute on all phases of the game." He paused and looked every single one of us in the eye, just like he always did. "Let's go win this game!"

That hit us in just the right spot. Now we were hyped! Not too high and not too low. We were still levelheaded, but hyped.

"Welcome to the FedEx Orange Bowl!" We could hear the man on the microphone as we finished our warm-up routine.

Bobby Bowden's team may have been the defending National Championship team, but by the night's end, they sure didn't look like it.

It was a battle that included back-and-forth interceptions that kept FSU out of the end zone and kept us from scoring all that we were capable of. But our defense forced them off the field on every single offensive series and refused to allow Weinke to throw for a single touchdown.

When we were ahead 6–0 in the fourth quarter, Rocky Calmus knocked the ball out of Weinke's hands as he scrambled out of the pocket, attempting to get away from our rushers. Cutting back to the left, I was able to recover the fumble. Just two plays later, Griffin ran it in for a touchdown, extending our lead to 13–0.

With just one minute left to go, we were forced to punt.

From the sidelines, I watched as the snap went up and over our punter's head. But luckily, he ran back, grabbed the ball, and ran it into the end zone for a safety. We didn't want to give up any points, but 2 points for a safety were fewer than 7 if he had allowed FSU to recover and score.

The seconds dwindled off, and some of the guys snuck up behind Coach Bob Stoops with the Gatorade cooler in hand. At 13–2, we were the National Champions!

The perfect season, 13–0.

Coming home after our win was surreal. Just two years ago, we had a losing season, and now we were the champs.

But keeping with Coach Stoops's mentality, the celebration

didn't last for too long. In short order we were back to work preparing for the next season.

My prep work looked the same. Practice, work out, study, and spend time with Coach Mike. He was my Picasso, and I was his blank canvas. Because we spent so much time together, I started to see things on the field like he saw them. We thought alike, worked alike, and even moved alike.

When the season started, my preparation began to show. I was dominating. No one could get past me, and even if they did, I was still going to catch them from behind.

The best game of the season came on October 6. The Red River Rivalry was one of my favorite games of the year because the atmosphere at the Cotton Bowl was absolutely electric. There was nothing quite like it.

Before I moved to OU back in '98, I didn't even really know where Norman, Oklahoma, was on the map. As a California kid, I didn't pay much attention to football on TV anyway. I was too busy playing my own games.

But walking into the Cotton Bowl is an experience like nothing else. The stadium is completely split in half, crimson on one side and burnt orange on the other. One side screaming one thing, and the other shouting another. I'd been here three times before.

"Boomer!"

"Sooner!"

"Hook'em Horns!"

The chants and shouts that originated from the different fans were both distinct and muddled together.

When we ran onto the field that day, some of us had our pointer fingers in the air, signifying that we were number one. But most of us came out flashing our upside-down horns for all to see.

On the other side, the Longhorns came running out with their horns up.

It's the same every year. Rank goes out the window and record doesn't matter, but when we cross the Red River, everything resets for the game that is about to take place inside the Cotton Bowl.

From the moment we kicked the ball off, the battle was on. Back and forth and back and forth. Woolfolk got an interception, but we couldn't capitalize. Our quarterback, Hybl, got hammered and had to leave the game. The first quarter was scoreless.

Second quarter, things were the same. Every down was a war. The crowd was screaming at a decibel that would have blown any speaker.

In those situations you have to keep a laser-sharp focus because you really can't hear anything while at the same time, you're hearing everything.

Texas marched the ball down the field and picked up a lucky pass interference call. The result of that call put them in position to score. But our defense came up big and stopped them. On their field goal attempt, it was Woolfolk who got the blocked kick.

Jason White, our backup quarterback, led our offense down the field with some killer throws and nearly scored on a gutsy run. Jason and Griffin got us six on the next play with the option. Meanwhile, on the defensive side of the ball, Texas made some big plays, but we fought right back every time. They had a real chance to get 6 points right before halftime. But our defense came up big, and all they got was three. We ended the third quarter with the score 7–3.

As we crossed over into the fourth quarter, White and our offense put together an incredible drive that took them all the way to the one-yard-line. After a penalty that set them back 5 yards, we had to settle for a field goal attempt. But Duncan missed, pushing it left, leaving an opportunity for Texas to get right back into the game.

Texas quarterback Sims put together an impressive drive, and we were fighting him back the whole way. But when the touchdown pass finally flew, Antonio Perkins intercepted the ball, keeping the Longhorns scoreless.

Our guys had another good drive but came up short. On fourth down and 16 to go, Mike Stoops had a stroke of genius.

"Listen, guys," he said at the sideline, "set up for the field goal but fake it and go for the pooch kick."

Our guys pulled it off perfectly, and Texas helped us out in a big way when Nathan Vasher jumped on the ball behind the 5-yard line, keeping it from rolling into the end zone.

Coach Mike Stoops said, "Hey, Roy, we're going to call Slam Dog Blitz."

Then he paused like he was about to say something else.

"Roy, do not leave your feet."

I had jumped through the air earlier in the game and had gotten hurt when I got blindsided mid-jump.

Slam Dog calls for Lehmen, the middle linebacker, to crash through the gap on one side of the center while the noseguard charges the other gap. Moving in this way would keep the Texas linemen busy and leave a hole for me to come busting through to get to Sims.

With just 2:06 remaining in the fourth quarter, Sims and company trotted onto the field to begin their drive, hopeful for a touchdown. We could not allow them to score.

As Sims went under center, we got into position. I crept into my place, ready to smash every dream of victory that Texas had. As I stood quietly, trying to conceal my position, I had a flashback to the tunnel in 1999.

"Ya'll are a joke!" I could still hear Major Applewhite's banter.

With my body in position to launch, I began to have an internal argument.

Coach said not to jump.

But I watched the film, and I know what they're about to try, and I know how Slam Dog can wreck their plan if we play our cards right. But I'm gonna have to jump.

There will be hell to pay with Coach Mike, no matter what happens, if I leave my feet.

I breathed in and out, still in my stance and ready for the ball to be snapped any second now.

No matter what it takes, I will not lose to Texas!

Then I knew what I had to do. I had to go with my instinct.

I knew that the ball was going to have to come out fast because they knew that we were blitzing.

Sims called an audible for Williams to move into a hot route, putting one of their halfbacks, Robin, in position to block me. But he was like five foot five or five six, and he knew better than to try to take me on up high because I would have just run him over. So I knew that he would try to cut my feet out from under me.

I have to jump, I said internally.

I'm gonna leave my feet, but I have to make this play.

I backed up just a little so that I could get a running start, and then I listened to the quarterback's cadence. Listening to his rhythm and thinking back over the entire game, I made my best guess as to when he was going to say those magic words that would snap the ball.

"Hike!"

On instinct, I shot out of my starting blocks. As I was flying through the air, my mind was whirling. *God, please let me get this dude!*

Milliseconds later, I hit Sims just perfectly, with my left hand on the back of his shoulder pads, and with my right I hit the ball, sending it fluttering in the air. The ball literally flew right into the hands of our very own Lehmen, and all he had to do was walk into the end zone for the touchdown. When I hit the ground, I was immediately flashing the horns down with my hand because I knew we just put the nail in their coffin.

I've never felt so alive as I was in that moment and, at the same time, so petrified about the conversation that I knew I was going to have to have with Coach Mike.

As I jumped up off the ground, I was celebrating with my team and simultaneously thinking about how I could avoid Coach for the longest time. I sped past the sideline because I played on special teams. Guys were slapping my helmet as I ran by, and the crimson side of the stadium was still going nuts.

Kickoff went, and we ran down there and made a great stop. Then I was on defense, which was fine with me because I didn't want to be where Coach Mike was. On their very first play, Texas was gunning for the middle, trying to gain as many yards as possible. I knew where they were aiming, but Sims must not have seen me standing there when he threw it—because the ball was coming right for me. I jumped as high as I could and snatched the ball out of the air, intercepting it. With just under two minutes left in the game, as I got up off the ground with the ball tucked underneath my right arm, I knew that I had officially extinguished any opportunity that Texas could have had to win.

Coach Mike came out onto the field to receive me as I walked off. He put his left arm around my helmet and almost held me in a headlock position for a minute.

"I told you not to effin' jump!"

I proceeded to get my butt chewed for going against his

direction. Only after he was completely done did he finally congratulate me for the interception.

Our offense couldn't do anything after my interception and we had to punt. But then our defense came back onto the field, intent to shut Texas out in four downs. We got the stop, sending Texas's offense back to the sideline with their tails tucked in between their legs.

White took a knee, and the clock ran out.

14–3, we won!

Winning against Texas was a sweet victory and definitely a highlight of my career at OU, but winning the National Championship is my proudest accomplishment while playing for Coach Stoops.

As the season's end came, I was deeply honored by all the awards that I received. It brought back all the memories of how football even became a part of my life in the first place. The hexagon and the games in the street seemed like eons ago.

That year I was awarded the Jim Thorpe Award as America's top defensive back and the Bronko Nagurski Trophy as the nation's top overall defensive player.

After it was announced that I won the Bronko Nagurski Trophy, one of my teammates called me.

"Hey, bro," he said, not letting me get a word in, "did you know that you're the first guy to win both the Nagurski and the Thorpe in the same year ever?"

I didn't know, honestly. If I'm being real, I wasn't expecting all the awards anyway. I just wanted to play my best football.

I even finished seventh in the Heisman Trophy race, which is quite a feat because defensive players are never ranked that high in the running.

Then lastly, I was honored as Consensus First Team All-American and Big 12 Defensive Player of the Year, as well as a two-time First-Team All-Big 12.

My time at OU was unforgettable. I could've played one more year, but I knew that the time was right for me to leave and go out for the draft.

New challenges awaited me at the next level, and I couldn't wait to face them head-on, just like I always did.

CHAPTER 9
THE DRAFT

When I announced that I was declaring for the draft, I knew that I had a lot to prepare for. I believed that stepping out of OU on a high note was going to put me in a good position to go high in the draft.

At first, though, I was just trying to figure out who I wanted to help me through the process. Most guys hire their agent first, but not me. The first person I hired was a financial advisor, and then I found my agent. At the time, Tom Condon worked with an incredible agency called IMG. They had a training facility in Sarasota, Florida.

So that's where I went. IMG provided a car for me. I stayed in a townhouse on the facility. They had three meals a day, even a snack or whatever I wanted ready and available. It was awesome.

We went to work right away. There were lots of professional trainers on staff because IMG managed lots of different kinds of athletes. The Olympic sprinter, Michael Johnson, joined us. He worked with us for three days when we first got to IMG to teach us how to run the 40-yard dash. Then before we left to go to the combine, he came back to help us fine-tune our bodies to their full potential.

When we weren't training our bodies, we were preparing our minds. IMG had a team that helped us prepare to take the Wonderlic AIQ test. The test is sort of like an IQ test. In this case, AIQ stands for athletic intelligence quotient. It specifically zeros in on an individual's intelligence and how quickly a person can acquire, process, and apply information.

At first, when I heard there would be a test, I was concerned. But the IMG team reassured me that the goal wasn't to disqualify draft candidates but to analyze the way a player's mind works.

"When they understand how your mind works, then they can put you in the best position that matches your AIQ."

"Oh, OK."

They even had a few mock tests for us to practice with.

The point of all our training was to be able to put our best foot forward when the day of the combine came.

Individually, we set goals for our weight, how many bench press reps we would do at the combine, how high our vertical jumps would be, and personal times for our 40. There were several other guys from other colleges that IMG was also representing, so we all trained together.

When it came time for the combine, Tom let me know that my schedule was going to be jam-packed. The combine is a chance for college players to perform an assortment of physical and mental tests in front of coaches, general managers, and scouts.

"Roy, please be sure and get some good rest before you leave because you won't have a lot of time to rest once you get there."

He was right. They flew us from Sarasota to Indianapolis, and as soon as we arrived, they took us straight to the stadium. Do not stop at Go, do not collect $200. We didn't even stop at a hotel to drop off our bags. Per their instruction, we went directly into these rooms where doctors of every type and specialty, as well as multiple trainers, began to see what they could see.

Every single NFL team that was thinking about possibly taking you in the draft had their own team of doctors and trainers. If you had any injuries at your respective colleges, the doctors and trainers would poke and prod at you for hours. Each team got their own x-ray and whatever other tests they wanted to run, all while you were still at the stadium.

"Are we done yet?"

I heard guys ask that. It was like the team of doctors and trainers didn't even hear their question because they just kept right on working. Some guys were there late into the evening, and they expected that you were going to be able to come back the next day ready to do your physical tests.

Luckily for me, I didn't have any injuries to report or medical issues to discuss. So my visits with the doctors and trainers were quick and easy.

After all the poking and prodding is over, you get to meet with the teams that are considering you in the draft.

I met with Buffalo, with Houston, and with a lot of other teams. But the meeting I enjoyed the most was with the Dallas Cowboys.

Walking into the room with the Cowboys owners and coaching staff was like walking into a scene from *The Godfather* movies. The room was not well lit, and it felt purposeful. It smelled like cigar smoke and sweat from nervous players.

Across the table were Jerry Jones, Stephen Jones, and Mike Zimmer. They didn't waste any time getting into the questions. They were drilling me.

Then Coach Zim took over the conversation.

"Are you going to compete in the combine tomorrow?"

Some people choose not to. They go back to their colleges and do the events required for the combine on their "home turf."

"Yeah, I'm gonna compete. I don't have anything to hide. If you like me, great. If you don't, great."

"OK, so *if* you come to Dallas"—he paused almost for effect—"what do you want to accomplish?"

I was being genuinely honest.

"So, I'm gonna play ball, but I really kind of want to start a foundation and impact the community."

He didn't look too impressed.

"I don't give a fuck about the community. I want to know what you're going to do for this team."

My eyebrows rose at his comment. I was being serious. I had been giving a lot of thought to all the opportunities that would come with a chance to play in Dallas. I really did want to start a foundation, but I knew now that was not the answer he was looking for.

"Listen, Coach, I'm in here because you guys think I'm a good player. If I come to Dallas, I'm gonna play ball. I ain't got nothin' to hide. I'm here to bring it. I ain't scared of contact, and I look forward to hittin' some people." Then I paused, just long enough to take a breath and look at how their faces were reacting to my words. "You've seen my film. You know what I can do."

He liked that response.

It felt good to be able to communicate in that room and be accepted. No one had picked me yet, but it still felt good.

Sitting there while they talked among themselves, I felt my mind wander a bit. I had trained my butt off at Sarasota, in Contempo, at James Logan, at OU, and now I was sitting in a room with the Dallas Cowboys Executive Team. Then I felt a small but noticeable smile come over my face. I really didn't care if they wanted me. I had worked so hard to get there, and now I was here to bare myself completely. I didn't need them to tell me that I had what it took because I already believed it for myself.

They thanked me for my time and assured me that they would be in touch.

Finally, all my meetings were over for the day, and I went to my hotel room.

The next morning, I got up early and went back to the stadium to compete in the combine. All day I just had a whole lot of fun.

My vertical jump was less than impressive. I've never been a big jumper, especially when compared to the other vertical leaps recorded that day. Sure, I jumped to touch the rim back in high school to make varsity, but this wasn't varsity anymore.

All in all, the combined events for me were not as stressful as I had been told that they would be. I had a smile on my face, and I enjoyed every moment. I knew that when draft day did come, an NFL team was going to pick me. I just didn't know which one.

Working with Tom Condon and the PR director for OU, Kenny Mossman, I heard rumors that on draft day I would probably go at the sixth pick in the first round.

What I didn't know was that Jerry Jones was working on a deal with the Minnesota Vikings and the Kansas City Chiefs. He had called them to ask if they were interested in taking me. When they said no, he set up a two-way trade. He agreed to go back two picks from the sixth pick to the eighth pick in exchange for Derek Ross and Jamaal Martin. Ross and Martin were good guys to get, too. But that put me back two slots.

In 2002 they didn't allow all the players to attend the draft ceremony in New York. Instead, they allowed only the top three or four. So I got robbed of that experience. But in an effort to send me off well, the University of Oklahoma put together an event where we watched the draft ceremony from the Barry Switzer Center. They actually hosted the event in conjunction with a recruiting day, so all their prospective recruits were there to enjoy the moment with me. But I figured I owed quite a bit to the school and to Coach Bob. After all, it had been he who walked me through the steps of deciding if I would go out for the draft in the first place.

When Commissioner Paul Tagliabue called the sixth pick, I still didn't know about the deal that Jerry had secured in the back channels between teams.

We watched as the commissioner made each team's announcements.

"With the sixth pick, the Kansas City Chiefs select Ryan Sims, defensive tackle, North Carolina."

Watching that, I was a little puzzled.

"With the seventh pick, the Minnesota Vikings select Bryant McKinnie, tackle, University of Miami."

I was just about to call somebody to ask what the heck was going on when I received a call from Jerry Jones.

"Hey, Roy, sorry about that. We just made some deals. We're taking you at the eighth pick."

"Sweet! Thank you, sir."

We ended the short phone conversation. And my mind began to run. *I'm gonna be a Cowboy!*

An ESPN crew was there at the Barry Switzer Center, and the camera was on me while I was on the phone with Jerry, and then it kept recording while we were watching the ceremony in New York. Even though I knew it was coming, when we heard the commissioner say my name, I got so excited, and the whole place where we were gathered went crazy!

Some of my boys from California had flown down to hang with me for the draft, and they were dancing. My mom, dad, sister, uncle, and grandpa were all there too.

I was hyped with my boys, hugging my mom, and then I looked at my dad, who was standing off to the side. His face was blank, staring off into nothing, somewhat unimpressed. It was the same look his face had made when Mom signed me up for football all those years before. Part of me wanted to do something about it, but honestly, I felt the same about him that I felt about the interview room with Dallas. I didn't care, but I did. I made it, and the only one who missed out on the joy of that moment was Dad. But I wasn't going to let him take my joy from me.

Jerry called again to let us know that my family and I were invited to a celebration in Dallas and that Jerry's own private plane was already waiting for us at the airport to fly us down.

When we got to the small airport in Norman, Oklahoma, there was absolutely no question which plane was Jerry's. It was the Gulfstream, and without a doubt it was the nicest plane I had ever been on. When we walked up the stairs to board the plane, I don't know what everyone else was thinking. But my mind was talking to me. *This is freaking badass!* I would never have said that out loud in front of my mom and grandpa, but I was definitely thinking it.

The flight down to Dallas was smoother than any plane trip I'd ever been on. When we arrived, it was apparent that this was planned out long before I found out that I was going to be the eighth pick of the draft. Jerry and I took a picture with a jersey, like we would have if I had been invited to the ceremony in New York. I met the equipment managers and the training staff, and we got a small tour of the immaculate facility that I could now call home.

Then we were done. I expected that we would probably fly back on Jerry's plane, just like we had come down. But when we were delivered back to the airport, we discovered that was sadly not true. They had a small propeller plane waiting for us, and it was horrible on the inside compared with the Gulfstream.

Dallas had been great, and the experience had been amazing, but the honeymoon was clearly over.

That propeller plane had me scared for my life. It was a roller coaster of a ride, and it wasn't the enjoyable kind. Everyone on the plane was holding their stomach, closing their eyes, and praying to God that we would make it. By the time we landed, my shirt was soaked with sweat from the workout my nerves were giving my body.

But we made it, and now it was time for me to move to Dallas. I was going to be a Cowboy.

Coaches Interview

CHAPTER 10
AMERICA'S TEAM

"Here! You need to learn this!"

Coach Mike Zimmer had just tossed the gigantic defensive playbook at me. And that was basically my greeting from Coach Zim when I arrived on the scene in Dallas. There was no "Welcome to the team, Roy" or "We're glad you're here." That's just not how Coach Zim worked, and that's definitely not how the NFL worked either. What's crazy about that is I didn't know. When you get picked in the first round, they expect you to start on the team right away. There is no grace period for the young guys who are only twenty-one or twenty-two years old. There is only "Let's get started *now!*"

I honestly didn't know I was going to start right away, so I was a little taken off guard. Since I didn't know, when I got to rookie camp, I started asking some of the other rookies for a bit of help. But there were multiple instances where a second-year guy told me to do the wrong thing on purpose to sabotage me. When I did it, then of course I looked stupid. But it didn't take me long to figure out that guy wasn't a team player. I never called him out for it, but I stopped asking him for help too.

If it hadn't been for Darren Woodson and Lynn Scott, I might not have made it through camp. Lynn was especially helpful during camp. He was from tiny Turpin, Oklahoma. I found it especially cool that Lynn was willing to help because he was a second-string safety, and now I was standing in his way of becoming a starter. But he was definitely a great friend to me and helped me out so much to get acclimated.

With camp finally over, my first preseason officially kicked off.

I was just twenty-one years old. August had arrived, and the humidity in Dallas is horrible! Walking out of the locker room, you're already sweat-covered, and you haven't even run a single play yet.

We were playing against the Oakland Raiders. I finally got in the game and got lined up in my position. But when the Raiders quarterback, Rich Gannon, got under center, everything started moving at light speed all around me. I couldn't keep up. In my mind I wanted to scream, *Time out! Yo! I need to get my bearings out here!* People were going in motion this way and that way. Nguyen, our middle linebacker, was calling to me for a check. I knew in my mind I needed to shift over. But my mind was everywhere but in the present.

There was no time for me to freak out.

Then Gannon snapped the ball.

Get to the ball, Roy! My body was feeling aimless, but my mind was coaching me. *Do the thing that you know you're supposed to do!*

Then I hit somebody, and just like that, everything in me rattled. Not in a bad way, but in the best way. *Calm your ass down. Let's go!*

It was then that I finally felt like I was ready to be a player in the NFL.

I was just a kid living out a dream.

Every time I walked through the locker room or ran out of the tunnel into the Cowboys stadium, memories would flood my mind of all the things that I'd been through to get there. At seventeen, I said, "I'll be playing for the Dallas Cowboys in five years." Looking back to that moment, I began to realize that I spoke out my future. The only thing wrong with what I said was that it didn't take me five years, but just four.

A lot of people had said a lot of things about me as a person and as a player, but regardless of what they said, I was living proof that things that sound impossible are possible. If you work hard toward your goals and you put in the leg work and the mind work, if you're willing to expend all of your effort even to the point of blood, sweat, and tears, it is truly possible.

If it had not been for Mom signing me up for that first team, there is no way I would have ever made it to this team. Every moment, especially in the beginning of that first year, I would find my mind wandering in gratefulness for all the things that got me to my present.

The first time I met Woody, I form tackled him hard. Too hard. Coach Zim had us running through a sideline tackling drill. In my defense, we were supposed to tackle one another. But as a rookie, I knew only how to go fast. If Ricky Bobby had been around, he would've told me, "If you're not first, you're last." That was my mentality. What I didn't know is that there is an unwritten rule that you should never, ever hit a veteran hard in practice. But going through these drills, I was too inside my mind, thinking.

All the coaches are watching, they're looking right at me. I've gotta perform, I've gotta keep trying to prove myself.

So, when I saw Woody lined up opposite of me, it was like I zoned out all the logic that I would have had if I was smart or should have had if I had thought about who Darren Woodson was. Instead of that, I lined up for a kill shot. Just like the kill shot I delivered in my first scrimmage as a sophomore on varsity.

The poor player I hit that time caught the ball, but he let it go promptly after I waylaid him. As I trotted off the field surrounded by my teammates, I was genuinely surprised when I saw him get up.

This time, with Woody, there were no teammates that were going to gather around me after the hit. But I did hit him, and I took him to the ground, hard. He did not like it at all. In fact, he was really, really mad about it.

Thankfully, though, he got over it and still decided to take me under his wing. For my first two years, I spent nearly every waking moment with Woody. I followed him around all the time. I just wanted to understand how to be a pro in the league. His wife probably got sick and tired of me being over at their house. But there were things that I knew he had that I needed.

"Woody, how do you prepare?"

"What do you eat?"

"How much do you sleep?"

"How do you do rehab?"

Darren Woodson was a phenomenal athlete. He was a three-time Super Bowl Champion and a five-time Pro Bowler.

All the little tidbits were nonstop. Every game, he was my constant coach, mentor, and teacher on the scene to walk me through every down. I held my own most of the time, but when there were moments where I needed a little extra, Woody was there. He reminded me of Ms. B from high school or Miss Hannah from fourth grade, leading me on and not willing to let me fail.

That first year I was balling, having so much fun. We didn't have a winning season, but I was hitting people, getting paid for it, and learning. Even though we weren't that good, I got to play every time the defense was on the field.

When the second season came, we got a new coach in—Bill Parcels—and we were playing some lights-out football. In the third game of the preseason, August 21, 2003, we were facing down the Pittsburgh Steelers. I hadn't seen them yet in my short tenure in the league.

By that time, I'd played some games, getting one season in the pros under my belt, but I had never faced Jerome Bettis. Jerome had earned the nickname "The Bus" for his large size and his running style. All 250 pounds of him would be running through the gaps in my direction, and I had to figure out how to take him down.

A preseason game is an opportunity for a coach to try out all his new guys, as well as give the crowd what they really want by letting the starters play a little too.

Finally, with just over two minutes left in the half, I saw Bettis lined up just behind Tommy Maddox.

"It's a run!" Reading their formation, one of my teammates called it out.

Pittsburgh never even shifted. They knew that we knew, but they didn't care because they had "The Bus."

"Twenty-five!"

"Twenty-five!"

Maddox wasn't in a hurry; the game was tied 7 all, and it was almost halftime.

The Steelers home crowd was loud, even for a preseason game.

My fingers were wiggling like little antennae picking up the slightest movement. My breath was measured, and my eyes were locked on #36.

"Hike!"

Then all of a sudden, something happened that gave me an advantage that I knew "The Bus" wouldn't be able to overcome, even if he wanted to.

My vision shifted, and I wasn't in Pittsburgh anymore. I was playing sandlot football in the hexagon back in Contempo. And I wasn't facing Jerome Bettis, but instead I saw Lloyd Greenwood burst through the gap, charging in my direction. He was breaking tackles right and left. But I knew that it was my job to stop him. I heard my childlike voice remind me, *You gotta break him down to take him down.* I wasn't intimidated at all. I'd tackled different versions of my impossible opponent a hundred times by now. I knew I couldn't try to take him high because he would just run through me like a piece of paper. I knew that if I tried to take him at the knees, he would just battering-ram me backward like an unrelenting jack-hammer. But if I took out his ankles and wrapped him tight, I knew that he would fall down like the big bus that he was.

It was an 8-yard carry, but I didn't get to him until then. When I jumped up off the ground, my vision snapped back, and I realized that I had just taken down "The Bus" on my first try.

"Attaboy!"

A teammate slapped me on the helmet.

"Let's make this stop, now!"

That's how I played. Every time I saw a player that seemed impossible to tackle, my vision would shift, and I wouldn't see him anymore. Instead, I would see a guy who was similar in build to someone I had already tackled. I would hear my own childlike voice: *You gotta break him down to take him down.* Then I would go in there and do my job!

We went from 5–11 in 2002 to 10–6 in 2003. In my second year, I earned my first selection for the Pro Bowl.

In 2004 Woody got hurt, and after a tenured career he decided to retire. I had Woody for two good seasons, and I definitely had him to thank for my early success. He had been the constant voice on the field for me. And when I knew he wasn't coming back, I realized that now that mantle would pass to me.

"I've got to be that voice now." Looking in the mirror, I heard my words come out of my mouth unexpectedly. No one was around to hear them except me. But I was filled with doubt about whether I was capable of being that voice. I've never been a vocal leader. I lead instead with my actions. I just try to be an example. Then the decision was made that Lynn Scott would play, and he was definitely a vocal leader on the team.

We would be in team meetings with Coach Zim, and for whatever reason we would not be picking up what he was putting down. Frustrated, he would shout, "Lynn, please tell these f-ers what and how to do what I just said!"

And Lynn would turn around from his front-row seat and put in plain English all that Coach had just tried to communicate to us. Lynn was smart. He saw football like the coaches saw it, and then he was able to apply his skills in such a way that he nearly always made the play. He didn't ever make the play like I did, but our different giftings made us a great team when we worked together.

Football was good for me, and it was good to me. I was making really substantial money. Truthfully, the money would have been better, like $3 or $4 million better, if Jerry hadn't made that two-way trade that moved me to the eighth pick in the draft. But it was still really good money and way more than I had ever made in my life before.

I was building my fan base too. Gradually I was becoming well known across the league. Every fan likes a good jersey, but usually the most popular selling jerseys belong to quarterbacks. In my first five years in the league, I had one of the top-selling jerseys out there.

My financial advisor called once to let me know I had gotten a residual check from the NFL.

"Hey, you just got a check for half a million dollars."

"Damn! Really? For what?"

"Turns out your jersey is super popular! You're in the top ten of the most sold."

The only guys selling more jerseys than I was were quarterbacks.

Life was good. Life was really good. I got to play the sport I loved for the team I dreamed about playing it with. I got to play on

TV, which meant my family got to see me even when they weren't at the game. My friends could come and watch sometimes. Dallas had always been my favorite team. It was my dad's team. My dream had become reality.

Football provided other opportunities too.

Right around the time of Woody's retirement, I started a foundation called The Roy Williams Safety Net Foundation. I built it to help low-income, single-parent moms.

We were able to help directly and indirectly nearly two thousand moms, which was awesome. We were focused on making sure that our moms received support, guidance, and assistance to enhance their quality of life. The reason I was inspired to do it in the first place was because my sister was a single-parent mom in college. I told her then that if I was ever in a position to help that I would, and the foundation made that possible.

In 2006 I signed to continue playing for Dallas. Our team's overall performance had been hit-and-miss over my first four years with the Cowboys, but I made the Pro Bowl in three of my first four years. So we agreed on a contract for $25.2 million to keep me playing till 2010.

Playing for America's team was like one big dream, coming true over and over again every day.

Everything was great, until everything fell apart.

CHAPTER 11
UNMOVABLE

don't think of myself as a naive person. I've been around the block a time or two. Living in a neighborhood like Contempo prepares you to have a "trust no one" kind of mentality. When your friend shoots you in the head as a joke, your vision of people tends to get a little jaded. But gradually, over my career of playing football in high school, college, and now professionally, my view of people had softened a lot.

No matter what business you're in, there are always imposters, supporters, fanatics, fans, and plenty of temptations. When I went from a poor college kid to an instant millionaire, everything I had ever wanted and all the things I had never desired came at me like a thousand Nolan Ryan fastballs aimed directly at me. Whatever it was that tempted a certain person the most was what seemed to be highlighted the brightest. Women, drugs, cars, houses, booze, parties, gambling, or whatever it was that was specific to them.

Playing in the NFL is not just about football. You enter an atmosphere that is very likely totally foreign to anything that you came from. You're going to become wealthy, and you're going to have to be careful who you choose to let into your inner circle. It's unfortunate, but not everyone who says they are for you are actually for you. Some of them are only out for themselves, and even though they can do an incredible job of making you feel like they're on your "team," they're not. They're leeches.

It's sad to say it, but sometimes those leeches can even be family members. When I made it to the league, I had family members show up out of nowhere that I didn't even know. It was crazy. The whirlwind of success and fame burns like a wildfire that carries the news of your good fortune to the far outreaches of every nook and cranny of the world, so everyone can know that you have something you didn't use to have. Not everyone is a bad guy, but there are more of them out there than you know about. Like with snakes in the grass, you don't even know they're right beside you until they strike.

Early in my career I was dating a celebrity, and she wanted to have security with her, so I asked around and got connected with a guy named Gus. He seemed like a pretty legit dude, and he checked out, so I hired him. When things didn't work out in my dating relationship, I ended up keeping Gus on my payroll to help me out with travel and some of the day-to-day. He took care of things at my house while I was traveling with the team and other things that I had him do.

I came home from an away game once, and Gus was waiting for me at the house just like he normally would be.

"Hey, Roy," he started. "You remember when you were telling me that you wanted to get some investment properties?"

"Yeah."

"Well, I got these two guys that you've gotta meet."

I should have known. I should have seen the writing on the wall. But I didn't. It was Gus. I didn't know that while I was gone on away games, he was stealing my personal stuff that he knew I wouldn't miss. I didn't know that he was conniving behind my back. I just didn't know.

A couple of days later, he set up the meeting with Mark and Jeremy.

"Roy, meet my friends Mark and Jeremy. Mark and Jeremy, this is Roy Williams."

So the meeting began. They talked a great game, telling me about an opportunity to buy into several investment properties at a time so as to make a greater return on the flip side. All we needed was a hefty chunk of cash, and we could start.

"The sooner, the better."

I should have vetted these guys, but I didn't have the forward-thinking to do so. The NFL does a decent job of providing its players with resources to do just that to help protect players, but I didn't think I needed to. I had Gus's word. And I had no reason to believe that Gus was a snake in the grass.

I took a couple of days to think over their proposal and plan, but everything looked legit to me.

So I called them.

"Mark, this is Roy. I'm in. Tell Jeremy that I'm ready for you guys to draw up the contract, and I'll sign it."

They were elated. And I was super pumped too. I had wanted to get an investment property for quite a while now, and this was going to be my opportunity.

When they had the paperwork drawn up, they brought it right over, and I signed it without reading all the fine print because, again, I just trusted them. It was a blind trust, but I figured I had Gus, and he had never given me any reasons in the past not to trust him.

"Alright, we got this. You focus on playing football, and we'll take care of your investment."

What I didn't know was that my signature on the dotted line gave them access to withdraw money from the line of credit that we had taken out at the bank I had secured with my money. All I knew was that we were going to do a bunch of houses at once and make a fat check when we sold them.

At the start of the 2008 season, I changed my number to 38. A teammate had that number when I first came to Dallas, so I went with 31. And 31 had served me well, but 38 is the number I wore at OU, and I wanted to get back into it. Plus, with my investment working in the background and the promise of the payout that it was going to bring, life was looking good for my future. When asked about the change, I told the press the truth.

"Thirty-eight is the number I wore at OU, and '8' in the Bible signifies a new beginning."

That's what I really felt was coming, an opportunity that would pave the way for my future legacy.

But then the fall of 2008 came, with both the season and the housing market crash. And it did crash, hard. It was like a kill shot that I was delivering to myself. It was the hardest hit that I had ever taken on or off the field.

To my horror, my signature was the only one on the contract as a guarantor. So, when everything went south, I had to pay for it. When I started to realize that I had been bamboozled, I tried to go after Jeremy and Mark, but they had filed for bankruptcy, so I couldn't touch them.

I found paperwork and contracts that I had not signed, but strangely they still had my signature on them anyway. Someone had forged my name. They didn't even do a good job, but it hadn't mattered much.

On the outside, I was trying to keep it together, so I wouldn't make a public scene. But on the inside, I was losing everything.

Nothing seemed to work even though I tried everything. I thought maybe I would be able to win a small victory to help with the debt load that was draining my net worth, but I couldn't. It was a gut-wrenching process to walk through.

I was just a kid living my dream until my nightmare started.

Thoughts of suicide lingered in the back of my mind, anything to help me escape this horror film playing out in my life.

I had allowed my identity to become associated with my wealth and the status that football afforded me. From an early age, I had always been unmovable both on the field and off it, no matter the circumstances that were around me. But in the heat of the battle, I was losing myself. I had trusted the wrong people. All the things that I had put such a high value on, that I put on such a high pedestal, didn't even matter anymore.

At OU, I just happened to be in the right place at the right time to make the play that would earn me the nickname "Superman." But when the housing market fell, all I was, was a broken Superman.

Life before had been so extravagant. Life after was just broken.

I hated it. But the further I got into those days and the more money I watched walk out of my bank account, the more I realized that I actually *needed* what had happened to me.

I had forgotten where I came from and how I got to the place where I was. Success was never my aim, until it was. Success had never been about helping me. It was always about me helping somebody else.

God had to strip me of my money to reset my thinking and redirect the trajectory of my life. At the time, I didn't understand all the reasons, and honestly, I still don't.

There were moments when God and I did not see eye to eye. And I was not too bashful to let him know what I was thinking.

"God, why is this happening to me?"

"God, are you there?"

"God, do you even care about me down here?"

"Hello! God, come on! Make it stop! Please!"

I've always admired Job in the Bible for his ability to continue trusting God even when everything was taken from him. But finding myself in my own version of a similar place gave me an entirely new level of admiration.

Right before I signed on the dotted line all those weeks ago, I decided that I would call my pastor to ask him what he thought about the whole deal. But when he didn't answer, I just went ahead and signed it. I was hoping he would say, "Yes, I think that's great," or, "Pump your brakes, Roy." It isn't his fault for not answering. It's my fault for being so quick to sign without calling him back to get a little outside wisdom on the whole deal. It's 1000 percent my fault, but I know that I missed an opportunity to talk to someone who would have been able to talk me down off the ledge of stupidity.

I lost everything that had any value in order to pay for the mistake that I made when I signed that day. My house had to be put on the market as a short sale. I had to sell two of my favorite cars. My Bentley was gone first, and then my Maybach SL60. All my furniture, gone. I lost people, friends that I thought were my friends but who hung around only because of the money. My status was gone. My life as I knew it was over. No more lavish parties or picking up the tab just because I had the money to do it. Roy Williams, as everyone knew him, was gone.

I watched as all my hard-earned dollars, which I had invested in the hopes of building a future, dissipated into thin air, becoming only a figment of my memories.

When all was said and done, I lost 95 percent of my net worth. *But ...*

It was in those impossible moments, those unexplainable losses, and those unthinkable difficulties that I made the greatest discovery.

I began to look back over my life, and every time that I did, it was increasingly easy to realize all the lessons that I was learning as I was going through the process. They say that hindsight is twenty-twenty, and they are right.

What I learned with Lloyd Greenwood was that even the impossible, and sometimes painful, situations aren't actually impossible at all. Football and life are the same. Football had prepared me for everything. I still had to make the choices in the moment, but the foundation had already been laid inside the 100 yards.

Respect always works for your benefit. First, you have to respect yourself, and then the authority over you—your coach, your teacher, your boss, or your pastor.

Teamwork is key. You've got to figure out how to be a part of a team. When you're working with people, you could be dealing with different nationalities or different personalities, but we're stronger together than we are apart. If you can navigate the locker room or the workroom with all that is going on, then you can be agile and flexible, and you can prove yourself in any environment.

Don't quit. You cannot even know the word quit. Any athlete will tell you that "I quit" is just a way to say, "I won't." No matter what comes up against you, you must be able to focus your mind and figure it out and then get it done.

Integrity is integral.

It's like I used to say about tackling: "You've gotta break 'em down to take 'em down."

Think about it: me sizing up Jerome Bettis to figure out how to tackle "The Bus" and you doing your next big thing are the same.

When I started, I never set out to become "Superman." But playing in the street, dodging cars, getting shot, running kids over, having to apologize, making varsity, getting recruited, learning to read at sixteen, passing the ACT, leaving California, going to OU, winning the National Championship, flying through air to tackle Chris Simms, getting drafted in the first round by my favorite team, playing alongside greats like Darren Woodson, becoming a great player in my own right, all of it ...

It did not prepare me for fame or fortune or even just a favorable future. That was never the case.

All of it built a foundation that prepared me for the fall.

Embracing my brokenness was one of the hardest things I've ever done, but it also released one of the most powerful lessons I've ever learned. The lesson after losing almost everything was the resolve to start over.

If I could use all that I walked through for something, it would be to help you know that you can walk through anything. No matter what is coming up against you, you can do it. It will probably still suck in the middle, and it may be hard or sad or even excruciating.

Just visualize your impossible opponent, remembering that the things and situations you've already conquered have prepared you in advance. Then embrace your own brokenness and be ... **UNMOVABLE.**

 **All Videos**